DATE DUE

Apr 26 '88			

JEAN JACQUES
ROUSSEAU

the social contract

newly translated and with an
introduction by Willmoore Kendall

A GATEWAY EDITION

HENRY REGNERY COMPANY

Eighth Printing 1971

CONTENTS

INTRODUCTION

HOW TO READ THE SOCIAL CONTRACT

To THOSE whose first question about a political treatise is "How much impact has it had upon subsequent intellectual and political history?" the writer on *The Social Contract* needs make no apologies. We know that thinkers as seminal—and as different from one another—as Immanuel Kant and Leo Tolstoy were moved by the measure of its thought, and believed themselves deeply in its debt. But for its influence, we are as good as told, there would have been no French Revolution, since the latter's leaders drew from it both their inspiration and their major ideas. From it, we are assured, derive some of the basic concepts—and thus some of the distinctive characteristics—of the modern democratic state. From it again, according to those who draw a distinction between democracy and rule by the greater number, derives the doctrine of majority-rule—and thus its alleged offspring, so called "mass democracy." And to it, we learn on good authority, may be traced some at least of the central ideas of modern authoritarianism and totalitarianism (for example, the idea that a man is free not so much when he is doing what he *chooses* to do as when he is doing what he *ought* to do), and thus, in part at least, the evils of contemporary dictatorship.

Now: Let us note that each of these claims is double-barreled: the book influenced men's ideas in such-and-such a direction and thereby produced, or helped to produce, such-and-such a political event or phenomenon. And let us, so as not to be tempted into a futile discussion as to whether a book—*any book*—is ever related to political events or phenomena in the manner the claims presuppose, agree to ignore the second barrel in favor of the first. And let us, by way of getting on with our job, fix attention on this patent difficulty: one and the same book can have influenced men's ideas in all these different directions only if either (1) it is itself a mass of contradictions and inconsistencies, or (2) large numbers of people have seen in it things that simply are not there. For, once we face that difficulty, we are driven back to what seems to me the key question, namely: "In what direction *would* it have influenced ideas if every-one had read it correctly?"

No one, I think, will challenge the statement that the critics of the *Social Contract* are by no means ready with an agreed answer to this question. For *Social Contract* literature is a literature in which every man's hand is raised against every other's; one whose characteristic mood is that of controversy and whose characteristic *leit motif* is the ill-concealed boast: "Others have misread or misunderstood; to me has been left the task of spelling out the correct interpretation; and here it is." Each interpreter, moreover, has his own answer to the question "What tendency or tendencies in the field of political ideas was the *Contract* calculated to forward?" as also to certain prior questions: "What, among the many theses and positions it sets forth, are its central doctrines? And what does any particular doctrine, after you have taken into account all that Rousseau had to say about it, in fact add up to?"

The main reason for the critics' failure to get together on an interpretation of the *Contract,* I hasten to add, lies in the book's own imperfections —or, to put it a little differently, in the character of the enterprise the author was attempting and the way in which he went about it. For it is a book whose author is evidently "sweating blood," by which I mean that he is presenting a line of argument whose ultimate implications he sees, if at all, only dimly—a line of argument, moreover, that he does not see how to bring off and knows he may not bring off at all. It is, again, a book whose author is evidently appalled at the amount of paradox and at least apparent contradiction in which, as he gropes his way forward, he is becoming involved. In short, the *Contract,* despite its engaging sentence-to-sentence simplicity, is an exceedingly complicated puzzle, which no critic has yet deciphered to other critics' satisfaction. And if different writers have found different things in it, and associated it with different tendencies in political theory, this is why: The book is in fact made up of diverse elements and emphases, which the author has not successfully integrated into a readily intelligible whole, and *may* not have integrated into a whole at all. Emphases reminiscent of the French Revolution rub shoulders in it with emphases that, at first blush anyhow, seem unmistakably authoritarian, and these, in turn, with emphases that appear to place the author in the same camp with the philosophical anarchists. And how they fit together, if it fit they do, is something we shall learn only when the book has been subjected—as it has not yet been—to the kind of textual analysis that patiently weighs every sentence against every other, that wrings from each phrase its last elusive scrap of meaning, and seeks—without, of course, imposing on the text the analyst's own ideas—*to help the text say* what its author was trying but could not quite manage to make it say.

Does this mean that the relatively untrained student, unlikely as he is to read the *Social Contract* more than once or to tarry over it when reading it that once, had best not bother his head much about it? Not at all. My guess, rather, is that the reader who approaches it without preconceived notions as to what it says and with a determination to keep an open mind on the issues with which it deals, can enjoy it and learn a great deal from it. For such a student will bring it certain strengths that the highly trained are likely to have frittered away in the course of their training, and that he can turn to excellent advantage—if he is willing to observe the few simple rules with which I am about to redeem the title I have given to this introduction. We might call them rules for reading *The Social Contract* with an innocent eye:

1) *Remember that a writer does not have to be ready with a lucid and unambiguous statement of a political theory problem in order to contribute to its solution.* This may seem curious to you, but the political theorist at work is as often as not a man driven by perplexity as to how to get into words a problem that somehow eludes the concepts he has at his disposal.

2) *Accept the statement of the problem in the opening paragraphs of the book only provisionally, and be prepared both (a) for attempts by Rousseau to restate it, and (b) for answers that bear no evident relation to any statement of the problem he has yet offered.* Rousseau's answers, in other words, may get out in front of his statement of the problem, and if they do you must be ready to help him out a little—for example, by asking yourself, What exactly is the question that this paragraph or section is attempting to answer?

3) *Do not decide too early in the book who, on Rousseau's showing, is "free" and who is "in bondage."* This means, for one thing, paying careful heed to Rousseau's warning, "This or that man believes himself the master of his fellow-men, but

is nevertheless more of a slave than they"—which suggests that being in bondage is *not* the same thing as being governed by a despot. And it means, for another, taking Rousseau at his word when he needles the English about their slavery between elections—an emphasis which suggests that Rousseau would have thought the French at least as unfree after their revolution as before it.

4) *Do not conclude too hastily that Rousseau is talking foolishness when he speaks of "forcing a man to be free."* Most of the cheap victories the critics have scored off Rousseau have been won by "refuting" him—and identifying him with the totalitarians—on this point. (Refuting him, incidentally, *may* be somewhat more difficult to do, without irreverent handling of the text, than the critics are in the habit of believing.) Note that on Rousseau's showing the man who is forced to be free is forced merely to keep a promise that he has made *voluntarily*. In writing the idea off as non-sense, therefore, we commit ourselves to the view that freedom is somehow tied up with the capacity to break promises.

5) *Remember, when you find Rousseau speaking highly of small states and poorly of large ones, that a man can recognize the practical inap-plicability of a conclusion to which his mind has led him, and yet regard that conclusion as both (a) valid, and (b) of urgent importance. Rousseau did indeed take it for granted that a return to the small state is out of the question. But this does not*

exclude the possibility, which I urge the reader to consider at least, that the central doctrine of the book is, quite simply, that in accepting the permanence of the large state we resign ourselves to perpetual bondage.

And, finally, 6), the rule that Rousseau—by implication—himself lays down (Book III, chapter i): *"I warn the reader that I have not mastered the art of making myself clear to the man who refuses to pay attention."*

WILLMOORE KENDALL

Yale University
25 January 1954

PREFATORY NOTE

This brief treatise has been extracted from a more ambitious work, which I undertook years ago without asking myself whether I was capable of seeing it through—and abandoned long since. Of the several fragments that it was possible to salvage from the manuscript, this is the least insignificant in point of length, and also the least unworthy, in my opinion, of being offered to the public. The remainder of the manuscript no longer exists.

BOOK ONE

NOTE

I PROPOSE, taking men as they are and laws as they can be, to inquire whether the political order admits of an organizing principle that is both justifiable and conducive to stability. I shall endeavor, throughout the inquiry, to wed that which right permits to that which interest prescribes, so as to reconcile justice and utility at every point. [1]

I plunge into the discussion proper without demonstrating the importance of the problem. Someone may well ask whether I am a prince or a legislator, and thus called upon to write about politics. My answer is No—and that that is precisely why I am writing about politics: if I were a prince or a legislator, I should not waste my time saying what needs to be done. I should either do it, or else hold my tongue.

I was born a citizen of a free state, and a member of its sovereign; *so that* however slightly my voice may affect public affairs, my right to vote on them is enough to impose upon me the duty of learning about them. And I am happy *to say* that I never turn my attention to governments without constantly discovering, in the course of my studies, added reasons for cherishing that of my country.

CHAPTER I

The Subject of This First Book

MAN was born free,[2] but is everywhere in bondage. This or that man believes himself the master of his fellow men, but is nevertheless more of a slave than they. How did this change *from freedom into bondage* come about? I do not know. Under what conditions can it be rendered legitimate? This problem I believe I can solve.

Were I to consider only force, and the results that it produces, I should say: As long as a people is constrained to obey, and does obey, it is acting rightly; *but* once that people is capable of shaking off its yoke, and does shake it off, it is acting even more rightly—for the following reason: Since in recovering its freedom it exercises the self-same right as the man that took it away, either it is justified in recovering it, or whoever took it away was not justified in doing so.

In any case, social order is a right—a sacred right, which serves as the basis for all other rights; *it does not, that is to say, flow from force.* Yet it does not flow from nature *either*. It therefore rests upon agreements.

Our task here is to find out what those agreements are. But before going into that, I must demonstrate what I have just asserted.

CHAPTER II

Concerning the Earliest Societies

THE OLDEST of societies, and the only society that is *in any sense* natural, is the family. Yet *we must not overlook the rôle of agreements even here:* the children do not remain tied to the father beyond the period during which they have need of him in order to preserve themselves. Once that need disappears, the natural bond is dissolved: *i.e.,* the children are exempted from the obedience they have hitherto owed to the father, the father is exempted from the duties that he has hitherto owed to the children, and father and children alike resume their independence. If they continue together, they no longer do so out of natural necessity but rather out of choice, so that *thenceforth* even the family keeps itself alive only by agreement.

The freedom that they *subsequently* enjoy in common derives from the nature of man, whose first law is to look to his self-preservation, just as his first duties are those he owes to himself—man being, once he has attained the age of reason, the sole judge as to the means of preserving himself, and by that very token his own master.[3]

The family, on this showing, is, if you like, the

earliest model of political societies: the ruler in the one corresponds to the father in the other, the people in the one to the children in the other; all, in both cases, have been born free and equal to one another, and alienate their freedom only as it is to their advantage to do so. The only difference is this: In the family, the father has his reward for the care he bestows upon his children in the love he bears them. In the state, the pleasure of giving orders takes the place of love, which the ruler does not have for the people.

Grotius denies that all power among men is instituted in the interest of the governed, and cites slavery as an example proving his point. His most characteristic mode of reasoning is to argue from fact to right. A man might use a more logical mode of reasoning, but none more favorable to tyrants. "Learned studies of public law are often merely histories of ancient abuses; and those who take the trouble to devote hard study to them are misdirecting their energies." (From the unpublished "Treatise on the Interests of France vis-à-vis its Neighbors," by the Marquis d'Argenson. That is just what Grotius does.)[4]

If we are to believe Grotius, then, it is an open question whether the entire human race belongs to five-score individuals or the five-score individuals to the entire human race. Grotius seems, throughout his book, to lean toward the first of these views. Hobbes takes the same position. You end up, on such a showing, with mankind divided into so many herds of cattle—each with its drover, tending it in order to devour it.

Just as the shepherd belongs to a higher order of being than his flock, so the drovers of men, *i.e.,* their rulers, belong to a higher order of being than their peoples. That, according to Philo, is what the Emperor Caligula argued, drawing from the analogy either of two fairly safe inferences: that kings are gods, and that peoples are animals.

This fellow Caligula's argument parallels Hobbes' and Grotius'. Aristotle also—and at an earlier date than either of them—held that men are by no means equal by nature—that, rather, some are born to be slaves and some to be masters.

Aristotle was right, but he mistook effect for cause. Nothing is more certain than that every man born in slavery is born to be a slave. Men in shackles lose everything—even the desire to shake them off: They cherish their bondage as Ulysses' companions cherished being brutes. (See a brief treatise by Plutarch entitled "Beasts Do Make Use of Reason.")[5] If, then, there are slaves by nature, that is because *previously* there were slaves against nature: force made the first slaves, and the latter's own cowardice kept them in slavery.

I have not so much as mentioned King Adam, or the Emperor Noah, sire of three great monarchs who, like Saturn's offspring—with whom some have seen fit to identify them—divided the universe amongst them. I trust my modesty will not go unappreciated: I am a lineal descendant of one of these princes, perhaps a member of the eldest branch of the family, so that—who knows?—if it came to a verification of titles I might well find myself to be the lawful king of the human race.

However that may be, no one can deny that Adam was lord over the entire world, as Robinson was lord over his island—so long as he was its only inhabitant. The nice thing about such empires is[6] that the monarch, safe upon his throne, has[6] no rebellions or wars or conspirators to worry about.

CHAPTER III

The Right of the Strongest

THE STRONGEST—unless he transforms force into right and obedience into duty—is never strong enough to have his way all the time. Thence the *so-called* "right of the strongest"—and, for all the ironical overtones with which it is asserted, its defense on the level of principle.

But will anyone ever get around to explaining to us what the phrase *right of the strongest* means? Force is a physical cause,[7] and what its effects have to do with morality[8] I am quite unable to understand. When I yield to force I do not perform an act of will but one of necessity—or, at most, one of prudence. How can it be my duty to perform such an act?

Let us, *however,* assume for a moment the existence of this alleged right. I contend that it leads to nothing but inexplicable nonsense, and for this reason: If might makes right, then the effect must vary with the cause. When might overcomes might, then, it succeeds to the right *which that might had made.* As soon *therefore* as one can disobey safely, one can disobey legitimately; and since the strongest is always right the trick is, quite simply, to act in such fashion as to be the strongest. Now: what sort of right is this that disappears as soon as the force behind it is taken away? If I am forced to obey, I have no need to obey out of duty; and once I am not forced to obey, I am no longer obligated to do so either. Evidently, then, the word "right" adds nothing to the word "force." As used in the phrase we are considering, it is entirely without meaning.

Obey the powers that be. If this means, "Knuckle under to force," then it is a good rule, but also superfluous: I answer for it that no one will ever break it.

All power comes from God. I admit that too. The same thing is true, however, of all sickness. Are we, then, forbidden to call in a doctor?

A highwayman jumps me at the edge of a forest. I must—compelled as I am to do so—hand over my pocket-book. But am I also bound in conscience to hand it over—even if it lies within my power to retain it? The pistol he points at me is, after all is said and done, one of the powers that be.

Let us agree, then, that might does not make right, and that we are obligated to obey only such powers as are legitimate. This brings us right back to my original problem.

CHAPTER IV

Concerning Slavery

No MAN, *as we have seen*, has any natural authority over his fellow-man, and might, *as we have seen also*, makes no right. We have nothing left save agreements, then, *to serve* as a basis for all legitimate authority among men.

Why, asks Grotius—if an individual can alienate his freedom, *i.e.* make himself the slave of a master—cannot an entire people alienate its freedom, *i.e.* make itself subject to a king? The question abounds in equivocal words, which evidently need some explaining. Let us, however, confine ourselves to one of them: alienate.

To alienate something is either to give it away or to sell it. Now: the man who makes himself somebody's slave does not give himself away; he sells himself—if only for his keep. But for what does a people sell itself? A king, far from furnishing his subjects their keep, gets every last bit of his own from them—and a king's keep, if Rabelais is to be believed, is no small matter. Are we to understand, then, that the subjects make the king a present of their persons, *i.e., give themselves away,* on condition that he shall take their goods as well? *Then* I fail to see how they have anything further to lose.

The despot, someone will answer, guarantees his subjects civil peace—*and that, surely, is something further to lose.* Let us grant the point. But how, if the wars the despot's ambition brings down upon their heads, along with his insatiable greed and the goings-on of his ministers, are harder to bear than ever their domestic squabbles would have been—what does civil peace profit them then? How if civil peace is itself a scourge—what does it then profit them? You can live peacefully in, among other places, a dungeon; is that sufficient grounds for being happy in one? The Greeks, while they were shut up in the Cyclops' cave awaiting their turn to be devoured, were living peacefully.

The proposition that a man gives himself and receives nothing in return is not only absurd; it is also unthinkable. The act in question is illegitimate and without effect—if for no other reason than that the agent is not in his right mind. To say that an entire people performs this act *thus* presupposes a people made up of madmen. And madness does not make right any more than *force does*.

Suppose, however, that each man is entitled to alienate himself; *there would remain the difficulty that* he still cannot alienate his children. They are born men, and *thus* free; their freedom is their very own; no one other than they has the right to dispose of it. Until they have attained the age of reason the father can name, on their behalf, such and such terms looking to their preservation and welfare. But he cannot name such terms irrevocably and unconditionally, this being contrary to the purposes of nature,[9] and beyond the rights of a father.

In order, therefore, for an arbitrary government to be a legitimate one, the people of each generation would have to be free to accept or reject it—in which case, however, it would no longer be arbitrary.

The individual who renounces his freedom also renounces his status as a man, and *thus* the rights and even the duties of human beings. There is no quid pro quo that can be given to him who renounces all. Such a renunciation is incompatible with the nature of man, besides which he who strips all the freedom from his will strips all the morality from his actions.

In a word: an agreement calling for absolute authority on one side and unlimited obedience on the other is both idle and contradictory. Over against a man from whom one is entitled to demand everything, one is, surely, committed to nothing: this single clause, naming no quid pro quo, naming nothing to be given in exchange— does it not, in and of itself, nullify the agreement? Everything my slave possesses belongs to me; what right, then, could he possibly have over against me? Any right he has is mine, and the notion of a right of mine over against myself—*which is what this comes down to*—is devoid of meaning.

Grotius and the other writers *I have in mind* squeeze a further source for the supposed right to enslave out of war. The conqueror, if they are to be believed, has a right to kill the vanquished foe; the latter is, therefore, entitled to buy back his life with his freedom—such an agreement being all the more legitimate because to the advantage of both parties.

Clearly, however, the conqueror's alleged right to kill those whom he has conquered in no sense results from the state of war. The relationship between men in their primitive condition of independence is not sufficiently stable to constitute a state of either war or peace; and for that very reason men living in that condition are emphatically not natural enemies. War is a relationship between things not men, which is to say that a state of war cannot arise out of mere personal relations: it arises, rather, out of property relations. And, that being the case, private war, or war between man and man, can exist neither in the state of nature, where there is no fixed property, nor in society, where everything is under the authority of the laws.

As for individual combat—duels and engage-ments *for example*—it does not constitute a state[10] *of war or anything else.* And as for private wars—*for instance those* authorized by the "Establish-ments" of King Louis IX of France and suspended by the Peace of God—they are excesses character-istic of feudal government—an absurd system if ever there was one, incompatible not only with the principles of natural law but also with any sound political organization.

War, then, is not by any means a relation be-tween man and man but one between state and state. It is a relation in which individuals are enemies only incidentally—not qua men, or even qua citizens, but qua soldiers, not qua sons of the fatherland but qua its defenders. (The Romans, who had a better understanding of and a greater respect for the law of war than any other nation the world has seen, pressed their scruples on this point so far that no citizen was allowed to serve *even* as a volunteer unless he had explicitly com-mitted himself against the enemy, *i.e.,* a specific enemy whom he actually named. When *therefore* they re-formed the legion in which Cato the Younger, under Popilius, did his first fighting, Cato the Elder wrote the latter that if he wished his son to continue to serve with him it would be necessary to have him take a new military oath:

his original oath having ceased to be valid, he could no longer bear arms against the enemy. He wrote also to the son, telling him to be careful to take part in no battle until he had sworn the said new oath. I am aware that the siege of Clusium, and other isolated data as well, can be brought up against me; but I am speaking of laws and usages —and the Romans, besides being the only people to have such fine laws, transgressed their laws less often than any other people.)[11] In a word: since it is impossible for a genuine relation to be established between things different in nature, a State can only have other States, never men, as its enemies.

The foregoing principle is, moreover, in harmony with the rules men have laid down at all periods in the past, as also with the regular practice of all politically-organized peoples. *For instance:* A declaration of war is a warning not so much to other States as to their subjects; and the foreigner—whether king, private person, or people —who, in the absence of a declaration of war against the prince *of a given state,* robs, kills, or captures the latter's subjects, commits an act not of war but of brigandage. This applies even during open hostilities: while the just prince takes firm possession of all public property in the enemy country, he nevertheless respects both the persons and goods of individuals; *in so doing* he respects the rights upon which his own rights are based. The purpose of every war being the destruction of the enemy state, one has a right to kill its defenders as long as they have weapons in their hands. But once they lay their weapons down, and surrender, they cease to be enemies, or instruments of the enemy, and resume their status as men; *i.e.*, the right to kill them lapses. It has proved possible, on occasion, to destroy a state without killing a single one of its members; and war cannot be the source of a right that is unnecessary for the achievement of its purpose. These are different principles from those of Grotius. They are unsupported by quotations from poets. They derive, however, from the nature of things, and are underwritten by reason.

So much for the *so-called* right of conquest: its sole basis is the right of the strongest. War confers upon the conqueror no right to massacre the conquered population; and the conqueror's right to enslave the conquered population cannot, therefore, be supported by an appeal to this right, which he does not possess. One has a right to kill an enemy only when one is unable to enslave him; the right to kill him thus cannot be the source of the right to enslave him. To oblige an enemy to buy back his liberty at the price of his life, over which one has no right to *begin with*, is *to conclude* an iniquitous bargain. *In short*: Is it not clear that we are reasoning in a vicious circle when we base the right of life and death upon the right to enslave, and then base the right to enslave upon the right of life and death?

But even if we were to take this terrifying right

to kill everybody off for granted, I contend that a man enslaved in a war—and, *by the same token,* a conquered people—has no obligation toward the conqueror save that of obeying for just so long as no alternative presents itself. The conqueror, by taking something of equivalent value with his life, did not spare him the latter: he merely slew him profitably rather than unprofitably. They remain— so far is the one from having acquired any authority over the other beyond his power to compel him—just as much in a state of war as they were before. To put it more strongly: the relation between them is an effect of the state of war, and the *continued* exercise of the right of war implies that there is no treaty of peace between them.[12] They have, to be sure, made an agreement. But this agreement, far from terminating the state of war, presupposes its continuance.

Any way you look at it, then, the right to enslave is nonexistent: it is not merely illegitimate, but absurd and meaningless as well. The words slavery and right cannot keep house together; they mutually exclude one another. The following formula—*which the right of slavery puts into the mouth of the master*—will always be nonsensical, whether it be spoken by a man to a man or by a man to a people: "I make an agreement with you: it is entirely to your disadvantage, and entirely to my advantage; I shall keep it as long as I please, and you will keep it as long as I please."

CHAPTER V

All Roads Lead Back to an Original Agreement

EVEN if I conceded everything I have refuted in the foregoing pages, the apologists of despotism would be no better off.

There is[13] a great difference between establishing order in a society and gaining mastery over a multitude. Let as many separate individuals as you please be bound, one after another, to one man: I see only a master and some slaves, not a people and its ruler—an aggregation, if you like, but not an association. There is no public good, and *thus* no body politic. Let the one man gain mastery over half the world: he is still a mere individual; his interest, distinct as it is from that of the other individuals, remains merely a private interest. Let him die and the empire he leaves behind—like an oak tree that breaks asunder and falls into a heap of ashes after being consumed by fire—at once disintegrates, and has nothing to draw it together.

A people, says Grotius, can give itself to a king. On his own showing, then, it is *already* a people before it gives itself to a king: *for* the gift is itself a civil act, calling for prior public discussion. In that case, *however*, it would seem a good idea to examine the act by which a people becomes[14] a people before we examine the act by which it elects a king. For this act, which necessarily precedes the other, is for that reason the true basis of society.

In short: unless the king has been elected by unanimous vote, what, failing a prior agreement, is the source of the minority's obligation to submit to the choice of the majority? Whence the right of the hundred who do wish a master to speak for the ten who do not? The majority principle is itself a product of agreement, and presupposes unanimity on at least one occasion.

CHAPTER VI

Concerning the Social Pact

THIS is my premise: men have reached a point where the obstacles hindering their preservation in the state of nature are so obstructive as to defy the resources each individual, while in that state, can devote to his preservation. This being the case, that primitive condition cannot continue: humankind would perish if it did not change its way of life.

Now: unable as they are to add to their resources, men can only combine and channel those that are at hand. Thus their sole means of preserving themselves from now on is to create a pool of resources capable of surmounting the obstacles, to set those resources to work in response to one and the same purpose, and to see to it that they act in concert.

Such a pool of resources can arise only out of the coming together of several men. Since, however, each man's power and freedom are the chief instruments he uses for his self-preservation, *the following question presents itself:* How is he to pledge them without doing himself hurt, *i.e.,* without neglecting the duties he owes himself?

This difficult question may be restated, in terms appropriate to my inquiry, as follows:[15] "Is a method of associating discoverable which will defend and protect, with all the collective might, the person and property of each associate, and in virtue of which each associate, though he becomes a member of the group, nevertheless obeys only himself, and remains as free as before?" This is the problem, a basic one, for which the social contract provides the solution.

The terms of this contract are dictated by the nature of the transaction, and in such fashion that modifying them in any way would render them nugatory and without effect: they are, therefore, everywhere the same, everywhere tacitly accepted and recognized, though nowhere perhaps have they been systematically formulated. Whence it follows that each individual immediately resumes his primitive rights, surprising as this may seem, when any violation of the social pact occurs; *i.e.,* he recovers his natural freedom, and thereby loses the contractual freedom for which he renounced it.

The contract's terms reduce themselves, when clearly grasped, to a single stipulation, namely: the total alienation to the whole community of each associate, together with every last one of his rights. The reasons for this are as follows: each gives himself completely, so that, in the first place, this stipulation places an equal burden upon everybody; and nobody, for that very reason, has any interest in making it burdensome for others.

The alienation is made without reservations, so that, in the second place, no more perfect union is possible, and no associate has any subsequent demand to make *upon the others*. For if the individual retained any rights whatever, this is what would happen: There being no common superior able to say the last word on any issue between him and the public, he would be his own judge on this or that point, and so would try before long to be his own judge on all points. The state of nature would thus persist; and the association would necessarily become useless, if not tyrannical.

Each gives himself to everybody, so that, in the third place, he gives himself to nobody; and since every associate acquires over every associate the same power he grants to every associate over himself, each gains an equivalent for all that he loses, together with greater power to protect what he possesses.

If, then, we exclude from the social contract everything not essential to it, we shall find that it reduces itself to the following terms: "Each of us puts into the common pool, and under the sover-eign control of the general will, his person and all his power. And we, as a community, take each member unto ourselves as an indivisible part of the whole."

This act of association forthwith produces, in lieu of the individual persons of the several con-tracting parties, a collective moral body. The latter is made up of as many members as there are voices in the assembly, and it acquires, through the said act of association, its unity, its collective self, its life, and its will.

A public person formed by other persons unit-ing[16] in the manner just described was in the past called a city; nowadays it is called a republic, or body politic. (We moderns have almost completely lost sight of the true meaning of the word "city." For most people, nowadays, a town is a city, a burgher a citizen. People fail to grasp the fact that a town is made up of houses, a city of citizens—a mistake that once cost the Carthaginians very dearly indeed. I have read of no instance in which the title "cives" was conferred upon the subjects of a prince—not even, in days gone by, upon the Macedonians, or, in our day, upon the English, though they come closer to being free than any other subjects. The French are alone in making everyday use of the title "citizens," and they *merely* because they have no real grasp of its meaning—as one can see from their dictionaries; otherwise they would be guilty, in appropriating it, of the crime of lèse majesté. For them, *be it noted,* the word denotes a virtue rather than a right. When Bodin made bold to speak of our citizens and burghers, thus failing to draw any distinction between them, he blundered enormously. M. d'Alembert did not make this mistake: he carefully distinguished, in his article on Geneva, the four classes—or even five, counting out-and-out foreigners as a separate class—in our town, of which just two make up the republic. No other French author, so far as I know, has understood the true meaning of the word "citizen.")[17]

The members of a body politic call it "the state" when it is passive, "the sovereign" when it is active, and "a power" when they compare it with others of its kind. Collectively they use the title "people," and they refer to one another individually as "citizens" when speaking of their participation in the authority of the sovereign, and as "subjects" when speaking of their subordination to the laws of the state. These terms, however, are often confused, *i.e.,* mistaken for one another, and it is enough to know how to tell them apart when they are used with maximum precision.

CHAPTER VII

Concerning the Sovereign

THE ACT OF ASSOCIATION, as the above formula makes clear, entails a reciprocal obligation between the public and *certain* individuals. The formula further makes it clear that each individual, since in a manner of speaking he *also* enters into a contract with himself, finds himself with two sets of obligations,[18] namely: those toward individuals, which attach to his membership in the sovereign; and those toward the sovereign, which attach to his membership in the state. The civil law maxim that a man is not bound by engagements entered into with himself is, however, not applicable here: there is a great deal of difference between an obligation entered into with oneself and an obligation entered into with a whole of which one is a part.

We must further notice this: because of the dual capacity in which the several subjects can be regarded, collective decisions[19] can create obligations on the part of each of them toward the sovereign, but cannot, for the opposite reason, create obligations on the part of the sovereign toward itself. It is, therefore, contrary to the nature of the body politic for the sovereign to impose upon itself a law that it cannot subsequently set aside. Since the sovereign can be regarded only in a single capacity, its position in this regard is precisely that of an individual entering into a contract with himself. Evidently, then, there is—and can be—no type of fundamental law that is binding upon the people as a body—not even the social contract.

This does not mean that the body politic is not quite free to enter into engagements with another such body as regards something that does not impair the contract. For, with respect to the outside world, it is a mere person, an individual. But *it does mean that* the body politic, or the sovereign, because it owes its very existence to the sanctity of the contract, can in no circumstances obligate itself, even vis-à-vis another body politic, to anything that impairs that original agreement—it cannot, for example, alienate a portion of itself, or subordinate itself to another sovereign. At the moment when it violates the agreement in virtue of which it exists it annihilates itself.[20] And out of *that which has become* nothing comes nothing.

Once such a multitude as we have assumed is thus united in a body politic, no one can offend one of its members without attacking it; still less can anyone offend it without its members' being injured.[21] Not only duty, that is to say, but interest equally, obligates the two contracting parties to be of mutual assistance; *i.e.,* the several individuals should try, under their joint auspices, to maximize the advantages the latter hold out to them.

As for the sovereign, since it consists exclusively

of the individuals who are its members, it has no interest that goes against theirs, and cannot possibly have such an interest. The sovereign power therefore has no need to offer guarantees to the subjects *collectively*, it being impossible for a body to will to injure all of its members. Nor, as we shall see later, can it injure them individually either. The sovereign needs only to exist in order to be what it ought to be.[22]

It is, however, quite otherwise with the subjects over against the sovereign: if it did not take steps to assure itself of their fidelity, it could not count on them, despite the interest they have in common, to discharge their commitments.[23]

The facts of the matter are these: It is possible for each individual, qua man, to have a private will contrary to, or *at least* other than, the general will that he has qua citizen. It is *also* possible for the urgings of that private interest to be quite different from those of the common interest; *i.e.*, his independent and absolute natural self [24] may lead him to regard what he owes to the common cause as a gratuitous contribution, *that is*, a contribution the making of which will burden him more than the loss of it will hurt the others. And he may, deeming the moral person that constitutes the state a fiction because not a man, successfully claim the rights of the citizen while unwilling to perform the obligations of the subject. If this sort of thing, inequitable as it is, were to become general, it would accomplish the ruin of the body politic.

To the end, therefore, that the social pact shall not be a meaningless formality, it includes, by implication, the following undertaking, in the absence of which the other undertakings it includes would have no binding force: Whoever refuses to obey the general will shall be constrained to do so by the entire body politic, which is only another way of saying that his fellows shall force him to be free. For this is the undertaking that dedicates each citizen to the fatherland, and thus insures each citizen against personal dependence of any kind. *In a word:* This undertaking is the king-pin of the political machine: None other can legitimize the *other* undertakings involved in civil society. Take it away, and these *other* undertakings would be absurd and tyrannical—a potential breeding-ground for the most enormous abuses.

CHAPTER VIII

Concerning the Civil State

THE TRANSITION from the state of nature to the civil state produces a quite remarkable transformation within man—*i.e.,* it substitutes justice for instinct *as the controlling factor* in his behavior, and confers upon his actions a moral significance that they have hitherto lacked.

Only when this transformation has come about does the voice of duty take the place of physical motivation, and law that of appetite. Only then, therefore, does man, who hitherto has considered himself alone, find himself obliged to act on other principles, and to consult his reason before he heeds his desires.

In the civil state man foregoes, to be sure, numerous benefits that he has been enjoying as grants from nature. So great, however, are the benefits that he acquires in their stead—such is the extent to which his faculties are mobilized and developed, such the degree to which his concepts are broadened and his sentiments ennobled, such the level to which his soul is lifted up—that we *are justified in saying this:* if only the abuses associated with his new condition did not often reduce him to a condition even lower than the state of nature, he would have to bless incessantly the happy moment that has snatched him, once and for all, from that state, and made out of a stupid and dull-witted animal an intelligent being and a man.

Let us reduce the items on each side of the ledger to terms easy to compare: Man loses, through the social contract, his natural liberty, along with an unlimited right to anything that he is tempted by and can get. He gains civil liberty, along with ownership of all he possesses. Lest we fail to grasp the extent of his gains, *however,* we must distinguish sharply between natural liberty, which is limited only by the individual's own powers, and civil liberty, which is limited by the general will—as also between possession, which rests either upon might or upon the right of the first occupant, and ownership, which can have no basis other than positive title.

Nor is that all: One might add to the gains from the civil state *that of* moral freedom, in the absence of which nothing can make man truly his own master. For just as motivation by sheer appetite is slavery, so obedience to self-imposed law is liberty. But I have already dwelt all too long upon this topic—besides which the philosophical meaning of the word liberty is, at this point, no part of my problem.

CHAPTER IX

Concerning Real Property

EACH member of the community gives himself to it, as of the moment when it is formed, just as he is—himself and all his resources, among which are the goods he possesses.

This does not mean that when he thus gives himself his possessions change hands and thus change character, or that they are transformed into property of the sovereign. On the contrary: Since the city's might is incomparably greater than that of the individual, public possession is likewise stronger and more irrevocable, in actual fact, *than possession as such*—though not necessarily, at least in the eyes of outsiders, more legitimate, for the following reason: The state, over against its members, controls all the latter's goods under the terms of the social contract, which serves as the basis of all rights within it. But it controls them over against other powers only by virtue of the right of the first occupant, which is conveyed to it by the *individuals concerned*.

The right of the first occupier, though less fictitious than the right of the strongest, becomes a genuine right only where[25] the right of property has been established. Each man has from nature, to be sure, a right to everything he needs. The positive act that makes a man the owner of such and such property has, however, the effect of excluding him from all other property. Once his *property* claim has been made effective, *that is to say*, he must confine himself to the property in question, and he *accordingly* retains no right to that which is held in common. That is why the right of the first occupier, though so very flimsy in the state of nature, is venerable in the eyes of everyone in civil society: respecting it is a matter not so much of respecting what belongs to someone else as of respecting what does not belong to oneself.

Speaking in general terms, the following con-

ditions must be fulfilled in order to make good
the right of the first occupier to a given parcel of
land: First, the land in question must not yet be
inhabited by anybody. Secondly, one must occupy
only that amount that one needs for one's subsistence. Thirdly, one must take possession of that
amount not by going through some idle ritual, but
by working and cultivating it—this being the only
evidence of ownership that, in the absence of
positive title, ought to be respected by others.

When we base the right of the first occupier on
need and labor are we not, in point of fact, pushing
it as far as it can go? Are we—*in other words*—
entitled to regard this right as unlimited? In order
for a man to put himself forward, once and for
all, as the owner of a parcel of common land, shall
he have merely to set foot on it? If a man is
mighty enough to put other men off that piece of
land for a single moment—shall this suffice to
deprive those others, for aye and ever, of the right
to come back to it? Where[26] the result is to deprive the rest of mankind of the living-space and
sustenance nature gives to all men in common,
how can a man or a people—without committing
a punishable act of encroachment—take possession
of, and so place beyond the reach of others, a vast
territory? When Núñez Balboa stood on the shore
and took possession, in the name of the Castillian
crown, of the entire Southern Sea, along with the
whole of South America, did that *indeed* suffice
not only to dispossess every last one of South

America's inhabitants, but also to keep out every last one of the world's princes? If so, the ritual was gone through a mite too often,[27] inasmuch as His Catholic Majesty had only to sit in his cabinet and take possession of the entire universe at a single blow—the sole catch being that he would subsequently have had to carve back out of his empire whatever other princes had already owned.

How the holdings of individuals, *physically* contiguous and pooled *by contract*, become the territory of the body politic, is clear enough. How the power of the sovereign spreads from the subjects to the land they occupy, and thus comes to be power over property as well as over persons, is clear enough also. This places the possessors in a position of greater dependency, and makes their very resources *serve as* guarantees of their fidelity. The advantage this confers was apparently not fully understood by the monarchs of ancient times: By styling themselves merely king of the Persians, king of the Scythians, king of the Macedonians, *etc.*, they showed themselves to be, in their own eyes, rulers over certain men rather than rulers over certain territories. The kings of our day, who know their trade better than their predecessors, call themselves king of France, king of Spain, king of England, *etc.* With so firm a hold on the land, they are quite sure of keeping a firm grip on its inhabitants.

The strange thing about this act of alienation is

that the community, when it receives the goods of the individuals who make it up, does not divest them of those goods. Far from it: it simply guarantees for them the lawful ownership thereof, transforming mere possession into genuine right, and occupancy into property. The possessors are, for that reason, *thenceforth* regarded as depositaries of common wealth, so that their rights are not only respected by all the members of the state but also protected against outsiders with all the state's might. And, that being the case, the said possessors have, as a result of a surrender that is advantageous to the body politic but still more advantageous to them, so to speak acquired all that they have given up—a paradox which, as we shall see below, is easy to explain in the light of the distinction between the sovereign's and the owner's rights with respect to a given parcel of land.

I have assumed, up to this point, a community formed by men who already possess goods.

Another possibility is that of *a number of* men who begin to unite *in a body politic* before they possess anything at all, subsequently take possession of a piece of land large enough for them all, and either use it in common or divide it up among themselves—perhaps in equal parts, perhaps *in unequal ones,* with the shares being fixed by the sovereign. On either showing, each individual's right over his own holding is always subservient to the community's right over all *the holdings—*

failing which the social bond would lack permanence, and the exercise of sovereignty would lack
genuine power.

I shall close the present chapter, and the present
book as well, with an observation that should serve
as the basis of the entire social system: the basic
pact, instead of *merely* destroying the equality of
the state of nature, does the opposite of that. It
substitutes a moral and legitimate equality for
such physical inequality as nature has been able
to produce among men—so that, while possibly
unequal in strength or wit, they all become equal
as a matter of contract and of right. (Under bad
governments this equality is merely ostensible, *i.e.*,
an illusion: it serves only to perpetuate the poor
man's poverty and the rich man's possession.[28]
Laws, in actual practice, are invariably useful to
those who possess and damaging to those who do
not—from which it follows that the social condition
is a benefit to man only when all own something
and none owns the least bit too much.)[29]

BOOK TWO

CHAPTER I

Sovereignty Inalienable

THE FIRST and most important conse-
quence of the principles established above is this:
Only the general will can direct the energies of
the state in a manner appropriate to the end for
which it was founded, *i.e., the common good.*

*But, someone will object, there is no good that
is common to the individual members of a society.
This I deny:*

What made the establishment of societies necessary was, if you like, the fact that the interests of
individuals clashed. But what made their establishment possible was the fact that those same interests
also coincided. *In other words:* It is the overlap
among different interests that creates the social
bond, so that no society can possibly exist save as
there is some point at which all the interests *concerned* are in harmony. Now: society should be
governed exclusively in terms of the common
interest *of its members.*

I affirm, then, that sovereignty is purely and
simply the exercise of the general will, and can

in no circumstances therefore be alienated. And I affirm further that the sovereign is purely and simply a collective being, and can be represented therefore only by itself—for the following reason:

While power can indeed be communicated *to another*, will emphatically cannot.

Let us look into this a little further:

While the will of an individual may in fact coincide with the general will on this or that point, it certainly cannot do so on all points and over an indefinite period of time. For the will of the individual tends by its very nature toward partiality,[1] while the general will tends by its very nature toward equality.

Still less can there be any *prior* guarantee that the two will coincide; it would indeed be a good thing if they always did so, but that—*if it happened*—would happen by accident not by design. The sovereign can certainly say, "As of this moment I will that which such and such a man wills, or at least that which he says he wills." But it cannot say, "Tomorrow also I shall will that which this man then wills." For (a) *to speak of* a will's putting limitations upon itself with regard to the future is absurd, and (b) no will can consent to anything contrary to the good of him who is doing the willing.

Where, therefore, the people makes a flat promise to obey, it thereby decrees its own dissolution, and divests itself of the character of a people. The instant there is an overlord there is no longer a

sovereign, which is to say that the body politic
is then and there destroyed.

This is not to say that the commands of rulers
can never pass for general wills. If the sovereign
is free to oppose them, and does not do so, we
must accept universal silence as evidence of popular consent. This I shall explain below.

CHAPTER II

Sovereignty Indivisible

SOVEREIGNTY is indivisible—and for the
selfsame reason *by which I have shown* that it is
inalienable: A *given* will is either general or it is
not. It is either the will of the whole people, in
which case it is an act of sovereignty and makes
law, or it is the will of a fraction of the people
only, in which case it is merely a particular will,
or an act of magistracy, or, at the very most, a
decree. (It is not absolutely[2] necessary for a will to
be unanimous in order for it to be general. What is
necessary is that every voice be taken into account;
which is to say that systematic exclusion of any
person destroys generality.)[3]

Our political theorists, however, finding themselves unable to divide sovereignty as regards its
source, divide it as regards its object: They divide
it into force and will, into legislative power and
executive power, into the power to tax, the power

to dispense justice, and the power to wage war,
into internal administration and the power to
negotiate with the outside world. One moment they
blur the distinctions between these parts, the next
moment they sharpen them. They make the
sovereign a being of fantastic properties, put together out of assorted bits and pieces—which is
like treating a man as if he were merely the sum
of several bodies, one with eyes, another with arms,
another with feet. One hears of Japanese presti-
digitators who, in full view of the spectators, first
hack a child to pieces, then toss its members up
into the air one after another, then make it fall to
the ground alive and put back together again.
Such, roughly speaking, are the juggling feats of
our political theorists: having dismantled the body
politic with sleight-of-hand appropriate to a fair,
they contrive, none knows how, to reassemble the
pieces.

This error results from their never having
formed precise notions regarding sovereign authority, and from their having mistaken mere manifestations of that authority for parts of it. Thus,
for example, they have regarded declaring war and
making peace as acts of sovereignty, which they
are not. Each of them, as the reader will see clearly
when we fix the idea associated with the word
law, is merely an application of law, *thus* not a
declaration of law at all—a particular act applying
the law to a specific case.

If we thought through the other divisions I have

mentioned in this same way, we should find that we are always mistaken when we think we see sovereignty divided: the powers we take to be parts of sovereignty are *in fact* dependent upon it; they invariably presuppose sovereign wills, which they merely translate into executive acts.

It would be impossible to exaggerate the extent to which lack of precision on this point has obscured the conclusions of our text-writers on political right whenever they have attempted, on the principles they have posited, to pass judgment on the respective rights of king and people. Anyone can see, in chapter iii and chapter iv of Grotius' Book I, how this learned man, and Barbeyrac, his translator after him—anxious lest they say on this question too much or too little for their own good, anxious also lest they give offense to interests they must conciliate—writhe and fret in the toils of their own sophistries. Grotius, who thought poorly of his own country, had sought refuge in France. Wishing *as he did* to curry favor with Louis XIII, to whom he dedicated his book, he left no stone unturned in his attempt to strip peoples of all their rights—in order to lodge them, with consummate artistry, in kings. Barbeyrac, who was dedicating his translation to King George I of England, would have liked to cut his cloth to the same measure. Unhappily, however, the expulsion—or, as he puts it, the abdication—of James II, forced him to proceed with circumspection, to dodge issues, to use equivocal language, lest he make William out to be a usurper. Had these writers only embraced the right principles they would have had no such worries, and would have adopted a consistent position throughout. But it would *then* have been their sad task to speak the truth, and they would have curried favor with no one save the people. Now: speaking the truth is not the way to get ahead in the world; the people appoint no ambassadors, fill no chairs at universities, and confer no pensions.

CHAPTER III

Can the General Will Err?

IT FOLLOWS from the above that the general will is always well-intentioned, *i.e.*, *that it* always looks to the public good. It does not follow, however, that the people's deliberations are invariably and to the same extent what they ought to be. Men always will what is good for them, but do not always see what is good for them. The people is never corrupted, but is frequently misinformed. And only when it is misinformed does it give the appearance of willing what is bad *for it.*

It often happens that the will of everybody, because it is looking to private interest and is *thus* merely a sum of particular wills, is something quite different from the general will, which looks ex-

These are the only sound precautions you can take in order that the general will shall always be enlightened and the people never misinformed.

CHAPTER IV

Concerning the Limits of Sovereign Power

IF THE STATE, *i.e.,* the city, is purely and simply a moral person whose life is in the unity of its members, and if its most urgent concern is its own preservation, then it must have universal coercive power—*i.e.,* power to set in motion and direct each of its parts in the manner most advantageous to the whole.

The social contract *therefore* gives the body politic an absolute power over its members, like that which nature gives to a man over his limbs. And it is to this power, where it is under the direction of the general will, that—as I have already said—I apply the term sovereignty.

Besides this collective person, however, we must keep in view the private persons who are its component parts, each of whom has a life and a liberty naturally independent of it. Our task, then, is to distinguish clearly between the respective rights of the citizens and the sovereign, and between the duties the citizens have to fulfill in their capacity as subjects and the natural rights they should enjoy in their capacity as men. (Let the attentive reader bear with me, and not accuse me too soon of contradicting myself at this point. Given the poverty of our language, I have *indeed* been unable to avoid a certain inconsistency in the terms I am using.)[7]

All that the individual alienates under the terms of the social contract, let us agree at once, is that part of his power, his goods, and his liberty whose employment is of concern to the community. But the sovereign, let us agree also, is the sole judge as to what is of such concern.

Every service the citizen is capable of rendering to the state he owes to it the instant the sovereign demands it. The sovereign, on the other hand, cannot impose upon the citizens any obligation that is useless to the community—cannot, indeed, so much as wish to. For under the laws of reason as under the laws of nature, no action takes place without a cause.

The undertakings that tie us into the body politic are mutual undertakings, and are binding upon us for no other reason. They are, *that is to say,* of such character that one cannot, in fulfilling them, labor for one's neighbor without laboring for oneself as well. If the general will is always well-intentioned, if everybody wills uninterruptedly the happiness of each, surely this is because there is no one who fails to seize upon that word "each" as his very own—so that when he votes on matters concerning all he is thinking only of himself.

All of which goes to show that de jure equality —*thus* also the concept of justice to which such equality leads—derives from the inside track that each assigns to himself, and therefore from the nature of man.

It goes to show also that in order to be truly general the general will must be general not only as regards its essential character, but as regards its object as well: It must emanate from everybody and apply to everybody, so that it divests itself of its inherent rectitude the instant it looks to a particular and determinate object. For where this happens we are passing judgment upon that which is alien to us, and thus have no valid principle of equity to guide us.

To put the same point in another way: The instant there arises a question of fact, or one concerning the right of an individual in a matter that has not been regulated by a prior collective agreement, the proceeding becomes contentious. It becomes, that is to say, a suit, with the interested individuals as one party and the public as the other—a suit, however, in which I *am able to* see neither what law should be applied nor what judge should hand down the decision. It would be absurd to try to resolve such a dispute by an express decision of the general will, which *here* can be nothing more than the finding of one of the parties—and, as such, nothing more in the eyes of the other party than an alien and particular will, which in the nature of the case leans toward injustice and is subject to error.

The general will therefore ceases to be itself[8] when it has a particular object, which is to say that just as it cannot be represented by a particular will it cannot, qua general, express itself regarding either a man or a fact. When, for example, the people of Athens—appointing and removing officials, awarding honors here, imposing punishments there—indiscriminately performed, through its particular decrees, all the functions of government, it no longer had, properly speaking, a general will at all; *i.e.,* at such times it was no longer acting as the sovereign but as the government. This will no doubt seem to contradict current ideas *on this question*. But the reader must give me time to set forth my own.

The point to grasp in all this is that what generalizes a will is not so much the number of voices *that speak out in its favor* as the common interest that harmonizes them. For in the body politic[9] each knuckles under, as a matter of course, to the terms he imposes upon others; *i.e.,* interest and justice coincide to a remarkable degree, and this confers upon the collective deliberations a quality of equitableness that is conspicuously absent during the discussion of any matter involving a particular interest[10]—which is to say any matter in which there is no common interest to harmonize and bring into identity the ruling *in the mind* of the judge and that *in the mind* of the *other* party.

Wherever we turn in search of our principle, then, we invariably arrive at one and the same conclusion, namely: The social contract establishes among the citizens an equality of such character that each binds himself on the same terms as all the others, and is *thus* entitled to enjoy the same rights as all the others. Given the nature of the pact, therefore, every act of sovereignty, that is to say, every authentic act of the general will, burdens or favors all the citizens equally. The sovereign knows only the nation as a whole, and never singles out any of the individuals of whom it is composed.

What then is an act of sovereignty, in the strict sense of that term? It is an agreement between the body politic and each of its members, not *therefore* between a superior and an inferior. It is a lawful agreement, because based on the social contract. It is an equitable agreement, because everybody is a party to it. It is a profitable agreement, because it can have no object other than the general welfare. And it is a binding agreement, because it is backed up by collective force and supreme authority.

Now: In so far as the subjects' subordination is confined to such agreements, they tender obedience to no one; rather—*in so far as they are obeying at all*—they are obeying their own wills, and only their own wills. To ask, therefore, how far the respective rights of the sovereign and the citizens extend is to ask: To what extent can the citizens— each to everybody and everybody to each—make commitments to themselves?

Clearly, then, the power of the sovereign, absolute and sacred and inviolable though it is, does not and cannot exceed the outer limits of the general agreements *among the citizens.* Clearly also each individual can freely dispose of such of his goods and his liberty as the said agreements have left him. Nor, this being the case, is the sovereign ever entitled to burden one subject more heavily than another—the reason being that this becomes a matter concerning an individual, and lies beyond the sovereign's competence.[11]

Once the foregoing distinctions are admitted *the following further propositions are in order:* *(a)* It is not true that the individuals, in *entering into and fulfilling* the social contract, are making any real sacrifice. *(b)* Their situation is actually better as a result of the contract than it was before. *(c)* They have not given something away, but rather made what is purely and simply a profitable exchange: an uncertain and precarious way of life for one that is better, more secure; natural independence for liberty; the capacity to do hurt to others for safety for themselves; their own might, which others were in a position to overcome, for a power that the social bond makes invincible. If they have pledged their very lives to the state, it protects those lives at every moment;[12] and when they risk their lives to defend the state, what are they doing but restoring to it that which they have received from it? What that they would not have done oftener and more dangerously in the state of nature as—in the combats that are the latter's necessary accompaniment—they staked their lives on the defence of the things necessary for their conservation? If everybody may be called upon to fight for the fatherland when he is needed, at least nobody is ever called upon to fight for himself.

In a word: Are we not better off when, for the sake of that to which we owe our security, we run a fraction of the risks that we should have to run, each for himself, were it taken away from us?

CHAPTER V

The Right of Life and Death

THE QUESTION arises, How can individuals, who have no right whatever to dispose of their own lives, yet convey this non-existent right to the sovereign?

This question looks difficult only because it is badly put. Everyone has a right to risk his own life in order to protect it. Does anyone accuse a man of suicide because he has hurled himself out of a window in order to escape a fire? Or because he has perished in a storm *at sea* although he knew, when boarding his ship, that a storm was not unlikely?

The purpose of the social contract is the preservation of the contracting parties. He who wills this end wills the means also, and these are inseparable from some risks—some risks, even, that will turn out badly. The man who seeks to preserve his life at the expense of his fellows must, in his turn, give his life for them when that becomes necessary. Nor is that all: the *man who has become a* citizen has ceased to be his own judge regarding the danger to which the law commands him to expose himself. When the prince has said to him, "It is advantageous to the state for you to die," he must die. For that is precisely the understanding on which, up to this moment, he has been living in safety: his life is no longer merely a gift he has received from nature, but rather a grant from the state, *which he holds* on terms.

The death penalty imposed upon criminals can be explained in approximately the same manner: One consents to die—if and when one becomes a murderer oneself—in order not to become a murderer's victim.

In a word, and this brings me back to the question raised at the beginning of this chapter: In *entering* this contract a man is so very far from disposing of his life that he is thinking only of making it secure. Nor need we assume—*in order to explain the death penalty*—that any of the parties to the contract is scheming to get himself hanged.

Each malefactor, be it noted, attacks the law of the body politic. He becomes, by reason of his crimes, a rebel against and a traitor to the fatherland: when he violates the latter's laws he ceases to be one of its sons and, in point of fact, levies war against it. His preservation is henceforth incompatible with that of the state: one or the other must perish; so that *when* a guilty man is made to die *he dies* less as a citizen than as an enemy. His trial and judgment are at the same time the proofs and the announcement that he has broken the social contract and, therefore, that he is no longer a member of the state. Now: since he has *hitherto* identified himself—if only by remaining within the state's territory—as one of its members, he must be cut off from it, either by exile as a violator of the pact, or by death as a public enemy. For a public enemy is not a moral person, but a man. And, *as we have seen,* it is in his capacity as a man that the vanquished is killed under the law of war.

But, someone will object, the condemnation of a criminal is a particular act. Indeed it is. It lies, therefore, beyond the competence of the sovereign —which is to say that it is a power that the sovereign can delegate but cannot itself exercise. My ideas do all hang together, but I cannot possibly expound them all at the same time.

Let me add that frequent punishments are invariably a sign of either weakness or negligence within the government. There is no evil-doer who cannot be brought to serve some good purpose. Nor does anyone have a right to cause a man to die, even as an example, save as that man cannot be spared without danger *to the state*.

As for the power to pardon a guilty man, or to exempt him from the penalty required by the law and imposed by the judge, this can vest only in that which is above both, *i.e.,* in the sovereign. The power of the sovereign itself to do these things is not, for that matter, entirely clear, and the occasions for its exercise are *at most* very rare indeed. If in a well-governed state punishments are infrequent, that is not because pardons are handed out freely but because there are few criminals. Where crimes are numerous, their sheer number guarantees that they will *increasingly* go unpunished as the state perishes.

During the days of the Roman republic neither the senate nor the consuls ever attempted to exercise the pardoning power; nor did the Roman people itself, for all that it sometimes reversed judgments it had itself handed down, grant pardons either.

Frequent pardons indicate that shortly no offender will stand in need of a pardon, and everyone can see where that must lead. But my heart murmurs within me, and stays my pen. Let us leave these questions for some just man who has never done wrong and *thus* never needed a pardon for himself.

CHAPTER VI

Concerning the Law

WE HAVE now created—and breathed life into—the body politic by means of the social contract. Our next task is to give it movement and will by means of the law. For the original act—by which the body politic comes into existence and is unified—leaves entirely open the question of what the latter is to do to preserve itself.

Now: The right thing for it to do, the thing one would find in a well-ordered state,[13] is such in the nature of things, and independent of human agreements. All justice comes from God; there is no other source from which it can take its rise. If, however, we were capable of receiving it from so high a place, we should require neither government nor laws. And while there is a *second kind of* universal justice, which emanates from pure reason, it *we cannot rely upon directly either, since it* gets itself accepted among us only to the extent that it is reciprocal, *i.e., embodied in agreements.*

The laws of justice, since they have no natural sanction, fail of their purpose here below, *at least* when judged by human standards. They merely accomplish the well-being of the wicked and the undoing of the just: the good man observes them in dealings with everybody, but nobody observes them in dealings with him. That is why we must have agreements and laws, which join rights to duties and direct justice toward its proper object. In the state of nature, where everything is held in common, I owe nothing to him whom I have promised nothing, and acknowledge as another's belonging only that which is of no use to me. In the civil state it is quite otherwise: all rights are fixed by law.

What, then, all things considered, is a law?

So long as people are content to assign a purely metaphysical content to the word law they will go on arguing and will come to no sort of understanding. Nor, even when someone has defined a law of nature for us, shall we for that reason be any closer to comprehending a law of the state.

As I have already pointed out, there is emphatically no such thing as a general will with a particular object. Any particular object must necessarily be situated either within the state or outside it. If outside it, a will alien to it—*as a will within the state necessarily is*—is not in the least general with respect to it. If inside it, then it is a part of the state, and there arises between the whole and that part a relation that makes of them two separate entities, the part being one and the whole minus that part another. But the whole minus one of its parts is by no means the same thing as the whole —*which is to say that* so long as the relation just described obtains there is no whole, but rather two unequal parts. And from this it follows that the will of one of these parts is not general with respect to the other.

When, however, the people is laying down statutes concerning the entire people it considers only itself. Any relation that then arises is one between a whole regarded from one point of view and the same whole regarded from another point of view, without that whole's being in any sense divided. Both the will that lays down the statute and the matter concerning which the statute is laid down are, in these circumstances, general. It is this *kind of* act that I call a law.

When I say that the object of a law is always general, I mean that the law never takes cognizance of a man as an individual, or of a specific action, but rather of the subjects *taken* as a body and of actions *defined* abstractly. While, therefore, the law may provide that there shall be such and such privileges, it cannot expressly bestow any of these privileges upon such and such a person. It can create such and such categories of citizens, or even stipulate the qualities required for membership in them, but it cannot appoint such and such persons to such membership. It can set up a monarchical form of government, and provide that the succession shall be hereditary, but it cannot elect a king, or designate a *particular family to be the* royal family. In a word, absolutely no function relating to an individual object lies within the province of the legislative power.

Once all that is granted, we readily see that it

is no longer necessary to inquire who has the power to make laws, since laws are acts of the general will; or whether the prince is above the laws, since the prince is part of the state; or whether there is such a thing as an unjust law, since no man is ever unjust to himself; or how we can be free and *yet* subordinated to laws, since laws are merely the expression of our own wishes.

We see further than since *the idea of* law includes both generality of will and generality of object, that which such and such a man, whoever he is, commands on his own responsibility, is not a law at all: even the command of the sovereign with respect to a particular object is not a law, but rather a decree—not an act of sovereignty, but rather an act of government.

I therefore apply the term republic to any state that is ruled by laws, whatever the form of government under which this condition obtains. Only in such states does the public interest hold sway and the public thing have a real existence.

All legitimate forms of government—I shall explain later what government is—are *on this showing* republican. (I do not understand the term republican to refer only to aristocracies and democracies, but rather, broadly speaking, to all governments that are directed by the general will, which is the law. *In other words:* The government, in order to be legitimate, must not be difficult to distinguish from the sovereign, but rather must be the latter's agent; and even a monarchy, if this condition be met, is republican. This *point* will be clarified in the next book.)[14]

Strictly speaking, laws are nothing more nor less than the terms of association of civil society. The author of the laws ought *therefore* to be the people that is bound by them; *i.e.,* the task of formulating a society's terms of association belongs exclusively to those who come together *in it.*

But how are they to formulate those terms? Are they to do so by common accord, by inspiration on the spur of the moment? Or does the body politic possess some organ *whose function it is* to express its wishes? And, *if so,* who will confer upon that organ the foresight it will need in order to embody those wishes in acts, and promulgate them in advance? How—*assuming promulgation in advance to be out of the question*—will it *even* promulgate them as they come to be needed? A blind multitude, often ignorant of what it wants because seldom aware of what is good for it—how would it accomplish, on its own, anything so ambitious and complicated as a system of laws?

In and of itself, a people always wills, but does not always see, what is good *for it; which is to say that* while the general will is always well-intentioned the judgment that directs it is not always an instructed judgment. It must be brought to see things as they are. It must be brought, sometimes, to see things as they ought to appear to it. It must be shown the right road, which *is the road* it is seeking. It must be made safe against seduction by particular wills. Places and times must be brought more nearly within its purview, and the attraction of immediate and perceptible benefits balanced against the danger of ills that are remote and imperceptible.

For there is this difference between a public and the individuals of whom it is composed: The individuals do see the good they are rejecting; the public wills the good it does not see. Individuals and public alike need someone to guide them. The former must be induced to will in line with reason, the latter must be taught to see clearly what it is willing. When the people has been taught to do that, its lights *are such as to* bring understanding and will together within the body politic—with the result that there will be complete cooperation among the parts and, in the end, maximum strength for the whole.

From the foregoing considerations there emerges the need for a legislator.

CHAPTER VII

The Legislator

THE TASK of discovering the best laws, *i.e.,* those that are most salutary for each nation, calls for a mind of the highest order. This mind would have insight into each and every human passion, and *yet* be affected by none. It would be superhuman, and *yet* understand human nature through and through. It would be willing to concern itself with our happiness, but would seek its own outside us. It would content itself with fame far off in the future; *i.e.,* it would be capable of laboring in one century and reaping its reward in the next. (No people ever becomes famous until its laws have entered upon their decline. Lycurgus' system of laws had kept the Spartans happy for no one knows how many centuries before the rest of Greece took any notice of them at all.)[15] *In a word:* Law-giving is a task for gods *not men.*

Plato, in defining the political or kingly man (this being the object of his inquiry in his book on statesmanship), presses the same thesis on the level of right as Caligula did on the level of fact. But if these writers are correct in thinking that the great prince is a rare specimen, what are we to say of the great legislator? The great prince has merely to follow the model; the great legislator must design it. The great prince is merely the workman, who assembles the machine and keeps it running; the great legislator is the inventor, who creates it. As Montesquieu puts it: When societies are in their infancy, rulers create the institutions of their republics; later on, it is the institutions that shape the rulers.

The man who makes bold to undertake the founding of a people should feel within himself the capacity to—if I may put it so—change human nature: to transform each individual (each being qua individual a complete and isolated whole) into a part of a larger whole, from which he in a sense draws his life and being; to change *each* man's character in the direction of greater strength; to substitute for the independent physical existence each of us has received from nature one that is moral and that we share with others. He must, in a word, initially strip each man of the resources that are his and his alone, in order to give him new resources that are foreign to his nature, and that he can utilize only with the help of others. *In short:* The founder's handiwork is solid and perfect just to the extent that the individual's natural resources are reduced to nothing, *i.e.,* snuffed out of existence, and *his* acquired resources become rich and permanent. And that handiwork may thus be said to have achieved the highest possible level of perfection where *(a)* each citizen is—and can do—nothing without the cooperation of all the other citizens, and *(b)* the acquired resources of the collectivity are equal or superior to the sum of the natural resources of the individuals.

The state's legislator is in every respect an extraordinary man: extraordinary—*as we have just seen*—in respect of his talents, but no less extraordinary in respect of his position. He holds no office, and *wields* not one whit of sovereign authority. His function, which is that of constituting the republic, is entirely unknown to the republic's constitution; it is a private function, superior *to*, and oceans apart from, the government of men.

For if it be true—*as I have intimated above*—that the commanders of men ought never to be commanders of the laws, it is equally true that the commanders of the laws ought never to be commanders of men. Otherwise the laws would be the servants of the passions of an individual, and as often as not would merely perpetuate his injustices; nor would that individual ever be able to keep his private designs from undermining the purity of his accomplishment.

When Lycurgus gave laws to his fatherland, he first of all abdicated the kingship, and in most Greek cities the custom was to entrust the task of law-giving *exclusively* to foreigners. The modern Italian republics have not infrequently imitated that custom; so has Geneva, and it has never had any reason to regret it. (Those who know Calvin only as a theologian are poorly informed regarding the extent of his genius: the drafting of our wise edicts, in which he played a considerable part, does him quite as much honor as the "Institutes." Until love for fatherland and liberty has been extinguished among us, we shall—whatever changes time may bring about in our religion—go on blessing this great man's memory.)[16] And if Rome in its finest days witnessed the rebirth, within its bosom, of every crime in the book of tyranny, and found itself on the point of perishing, this was because of its having lodged legislative and sovereign authority in the same persons. (Even so, the decemvirs never arrogated to themselves the power to cause a law to be passed on their own authority. "Not one word of what we are proposing"—so it was their custom to address the people—"can become law without your consent. Romans, be yourselves the authors of the laws that are to make you happy.")

He who drafts the laws has, then, or should have, no power to legislate. The people itself, moreover, is not entitled to divest itself of this non-transferable power even if it wills to do so, and for this reason: According to the basic contract, only the general will can impose obligations upon individuals, and there is no way to be sure that the will of an individual coincides with the general will until it has been submitted to a free vote of the people. I have said as much above; but it is not idle to repeat it here.

What we find, then, is that the mission of the legislator involves two things that appear to be incompatible: an enterprise beyond human capacity on the one hand, and—for its accomplishment—an authority that is as nothing.

A further difficulty merits our attention: The wise man, if he tries to speak to ordinary people in his own idiom rather than theirs, cannot possibly make himself understood. There are, however, countless ideas that defy translation into the people's idiom: highly abstract concepts cannot be expressed in it; neither can purposes that are very remote.

The individual, *moreover,* has no taste for any

plan of government that fails to appeal to his private interest; and since he does not, he perceives with difficulty the advantages to be derived from the never-ending sacrifices that good laws impose. *In a word:* In order for a people still a-borning to cherish sound principles of politics, and *consistently* follow the basic rules deriving from reason of state, effect would need to be capable of becoming cause, and the social spirit that the laws are to produce would need to preside over their giving. Men would need to be, prior to the laws, what they are to become through them. That is why the legislator, unable as he is to resort either to force or to reasoning, appeals necessarily to another kind of authority, which can lead without compelling and persuade without convincing.

There you have the reason that has forced the founders of nations in every age to have recourse to intervention from on high, and to attribute to the gods the wisdom that is *in fact* their own. They do this in order that their peoples, subordinating themselves to the laws of the state as to the laws of nature, and recognizing that one and the same power is at work in the formation of man and that of the city, shall obey and yet remain free, and shall bear with docility the yoke of the public good.

The legislator appeals to divine authority, *then,* in order to carry with him those on whom human prudence would have no effect; *but* the judgment he *thus* puts into the mouths of immortals are those of a superior wisdom that soars beyond the grasp of ordinary men. ("The fact is," writes Machiavelli in Book I, chapter xi of "The Discourses," "no people has ever had a giver of fundamental laws who did not have recourse to God, since otherwise the laws would fail of acceptance. This is because many good things are known to the wise man that do not, in and of themselves, afford such obvious grounds as to convince others.") [17]

It is not, however, given to every man to make gods talk, or to get himself believed when he declares himself their spokesman. The legislator's mission must, therefore, be validated by the unquestionable miracle of his own great spirit. Anybody can chisel tablets of stone, or bribe an oracle, or feign secret communication with some divinity, or train a bird to whisper in his ear, or invent this or that other crude device for putting upon the people; *but* the man whose knowledge stops there, though he may indeed bring together—with luck —a bunch of fools, will never found an empire— nor will the crazy thing he has built survive his own early death. Meaningless stunts create a social tie that binds for a little while; only wisdom can make it continue to bind. The Judaic law, which has survived into our own day, the law of the child of Ishmael, which has for ten centuries governed half the world—both bear present testimony to the greatness of the men who drafted them. [18] And if prideful philosophy, or blind partisan spirit, continues to regard them as lucky charlatans, true political theory admires—in the institutions they launched—the magnificent and forceful genius that presides over the giving of laws that endure.

It is not necessary to conclude from all this, as Warburton does, that our politics and our religion serve one and the same purpose, but rather that during each nation's infancy the one acts as the other's instrument.

CHAPTER VIII

Concerning the People

THE ARCHITECT, before building a large edifice, studies and probes the ground it is to occupy, to find out whether it is capable of supporting so great a weight. The wise legislator, similarly, starts out not by drafting laws good in and of themselves, but rather by finding out whether the people for whom he intends them is capable of bearing them. That is why Plato refused to give laws to the Arcadians and the Cyrenians: he knew both were rich, and *thus* could not stomach a regime of equality. It is also why Crete was a city of good laws and wicked men: the people Minos had disciplined was, quite simply, a people loaded down with vices.

Many a nation has performed brilliantly on the world's stage that could never have knuckled under to good laws; and even those that could had only a brief interval of their history in which to do so. Most peoples, like most individuals, are malleable only during youth, and become increasingly incorrigible as they grow older. Once a people's customs are formed, once its prejudices have put down roots, any attempt to reform it is, *therefore,* a dangerous venture—and a futile one as well: it cannot bear to have anyone lay hands on its diseased parts, *even* to cure them[19]—just as some foolish, timid patients tremble at the sight of the doctor.

This is not to deny that we sometimes find, in the history of states, epochs of disturbance during which revolutions do to peoples what certain crises do to individuals (there are illnesses that put a man out of his mind, and deprive him of all recollection of the past). Horror of the past takes the form of loss of memory, and the state—consumed by civil wars, and rising, so to speak, out of its own ashes—frees itself from death's embrace and takes on anew the vigor of youth. Such was the condition of Sparta in Lycurgus' time; such the condition of Rome after the Tarquins; and such, a little closer home, the condition of Holland and Switzerland following the expulsion of their tyrants.

Such turns of events are rare: they are exceptions, the reason for which is always to be sought in the peculiar constitution of the state in which they occur. No such thing, moreover, could possibly happen twice to one and the same people: any people that has not passed beyond barbarism can still make itself free, but none can do so once the spring of its civil life is spent. From that point on a people can be destroyed by its *internal* conflicts, but cannot be restored by a revolution: once its irons are shattered it falls apart and ceases to exist, and what it needs thenceforth is an overlord not a liberator.

Remember this maxim, free peoples *of the world*: it is possible to win liberty, impossible to recover it.

I speak of youth, not infancy. In a nation's life as in a man's there is a time of *what I have here called* youth or, if you prefer, maturity, prior to which we can subject neither to laws. The moment at which a people has become mature, on the other hand, is not always easy to recognize; and the operation, if attempted prematurely, always goes wrong. One people can be given laws when it is a-borning, another cannot be given them at the end of its tenth century.

The Russians, *for example,* will never be a genuine body politic: they were given laws too soon. The genius Peter brought to his task was that of the imitator. True genius, the creative kind that starts with nothing and accomplishes all, he did not possess. Some of his policies, certainly, were well enough; most were quite wide of the mark. His was a barbarian people; that much he perceived—without, however, recognizing that it was not ripe for laws. He tried to civilize it—at a time when what it needed was hardening. He set out to produce Germans and Englishmen—when he should have made it his first task to produce Russians. He kept his subjects from becoming what they might have been—by persuading them that they were what they were not. French tutors give their pupils this same kind of training: they shine brilliantly as children, then live out their lives without accomplishing anything whatever.

The Russian empire will attempt, some day, to enslave Europe, and will itself be enslaved. The Tartars, today the Russians' subjects and neighbors, will become their rulers—and ours also. That upheaval seems to me unavoidable—besides which all the kings of Europe are working hand-in-hand to hasten its coming.

CHAPTER IX

Continuation

NATURE has put upper and lower limits upon the stature of a well-built man, and above and below these limits it produces only giants and dwarfs. There are, from the standpoint of the state's ideal constitution, similar limits upon the area it can cover without becoming too big to be well-governed or too tiny to preserve itself by its own efforts. For each body politic there is a point of maximum strength, which it cannot possibly exceed, and from which, in many cases, it *accord-*

ingly finds itself further and further removed as it increases in size. The social bond grows weaker as it is stretched. Thus a small state is, as a general proposition, stronger relatively speaking than a large one.

Numerous arguments may be cited as proof of the principle just set forth: In the first place, administration becomes more burdensome when carried on over great distances, just as a weight gets heavier as we increase the length of the lever arm on its side of the fulcrum.[20] It becomes more burdensome, again, as the number of levels of government multiplies: each town must have an administration, for which the people *must* foot the bill; every district must have one, for which the people *must* foot it once again; so too each province and each of the grand subdivisions, the satrapies and vice-royalties. These must, *I repeat,* all be paid for out of the pockets of the unfortunate people—and more dearly at each rung on the ladder than on that just below. We have, finally, the administrative apparatus at the very top, the cost of which is staggering.

The numerous surcharges I have just mentioned represent a constant drain upon the *resources of the* subjects; and, far from being better governed by all these different authorities, they are worse governed than they would be if there were a single authority for them to look up to. They have, meanwhile, hardly any resources left for emergencies; and each time they must tap such resources the state finds ruin staring it in the face.

Nor is that all: The government *of a large state* moves less vigorously and promptly to enforce the laws, to abate nuisances, to correct abuses, and to prevent seditious activities, which can be got under way in distant places. The subjects, furthermore, feel less affection for their rulers, whom they never lay eyes on, for the fatherland, which *because so large* is indistinguishable in their eyes from the whole world, and for their fellow-citizens, few of whom they even know. One and the same *body of* law cannot possibly be suited to so many provinces which are dissimilar in character, which, that is to say, have different customs and contrasting climates and are *thus* incapable of accepting one and the same form of government. Having different laws *from province to province, on the other hand,* can result only in trouble and confusion for the population: living under the same rulers, and constantly brushing shoulders with one another, they move and marry back and forth, and in doing so find themselves up against new customs—so that they never know whether their patrimony actually belongs to them or not.

Again: The seat of the supreme administration brings together in one and the same place a vast number of mutual strangers, among whom talents go unused, virtues unnoticed, and vices unpunished. The rulers, so overwhelmed are they with affairs, see nothing with their own eyes, so that the actual governing is done by clerks.

One final point: officials in distant places try either to put themselves beyond the reach of, or to control, the central government,[21] and measures must be taken to maintain its authority. These measures absorb all the public energies: none are left for *promoting* the happiness of the people, and almost none *even* for defense, when the need for it arises.

A state too big for its constitution, thus borne down by its own weight, collapses and disappears.

If, on the other hand, the state is to be sturdy enough to stand the jolts it is sure to get, and to put forth the efforts it will be obliged to put forth in order to sustain itself, it must provide itself a certain breadth of base. All peoples have, so to speak, their own centrifugal force, because of which they tend, like Descartes' vortices, to expand at the expense of their neighbors. They are constantly running afoul of one another, and weak states, in consequence, are forever in danger of being quickly swallowed up. Save *then* as a state establishes a kind of equilibrium with all other states, one that will approximately equalize the pressure all the way 'round, it is well-nigh impossible for it to preserve itself.

It is evident from the above that there are reasons for expanding frontiers and reasons for contracting them. *Now:* Striking the balance between these two sets of reasons that is most favorable to the state's preservation is not the least of the statesman's skills. Speaking in general terms, *however,* we may say that the first of the two sets, because merely external and relative, should be subordinated to the reasons on the other side, which are internal and absolute. Before all else we must seek a constitution that is sound and strong. And we should rely rather upon the vigor engendered by a good government than upon the resources provided by a large territory.

One further point: There have been states so ordered that the need for conquests was part and parcel of their constitutions, *i.e.,* states so ordered that they were obliged to be always expanding in order to keep themselves going. These states have, perhaps, heartily congratulated themselves upon *possessing* a need *whose satisfaction is* so pleasant. But what that need held out to them—at the end of their time of greatness—was their inevitable downfall.

CHAPTER X

Continuation

A BODY POLITIC can be measured by either of two yardsticks:[22] territorial extension and population. These two things can be brought into a relation with one another that is calculated to give the state the area it truly needs.[23]

This relation obtains where there is as much land as is needed to support the population, and as

much population as the land can sustain; for what
makes a state is men, and what provides nourish-
ment for men is land. Maximum strength for a
given number of people is a matter of fulfilling
these conditions.[24] If there is too much land its
defense will be burdensome, its cultivation inadequate, and its produce redundant—a state of affairs that leads directly to defensive war. If there
is too little land the state finds itself at the mercy
of its neighbors for the additional supplies[25] it
needs—which leads directly to offensive war.

Any people so situated, *therefore,* that it is obliged
to choose between commerce and war is by that
same token a weak state: It is dependent both upon
its neighbors and upon the course of events, so
that its existence cannot be other than uncertain
and brief. Either it subjugates *other states,* thus
changing its situation, or it is subjugated and put
out of the running. *In a word:* It can keep itself
free only by becoming smaller or by becoming
larger.

It is impossible to formulate in mathematical
terms any fixed ratio between the area and population that just suffice for one another. This is partly
because of differences in the quality of land, dif-
fering degrees of fertility, differences in the character of the product, and differences attributable
to climate. It is partly because of the observable
differences in the temperament of the inhabitants:
some live on fertile land but consume little; others
live on unproductive land but consume much. We

must bear in mind also the greater or lesser fecundity of women, the terrain characteristics that are more or less favorable to growth of population, and the extent to which the legislator can expect to contribute to the latter by means of the institutions he founds. The legislator, that is to say, should base his judgment not on what he sees but on what he foresees: he should pay less attention to the present level of the population than to that to which, in the course of natural events, it will rise or fall.

Finally, a peculiar topography quite often makes it necessary, or at least possible, to take in more territory than would otherwise seem to be required. Thus where the terrain is mountainous, or where the things nature produces—timber, for instance, or pasturage—are such as to call for relatively little labor, or where the record shows that the women are more fecund than those of the plains, or where the amount of sloping land is so great as to leave only a small area of level ground (which is all that counts as far as vegetation is concerned), people will spread out a good deal. Along the seashore, however—even where there are rocks and well-nigh sterile sands—people can draw closer together. The fish they will catch will make up, in large part, for deficiencies in the product of the land. They need to be closer together in order to fend off pirates. And, quite apart from all that, it is easier for them, by means of colonies, to slough off any surplus population.

We must now add, to our list of presuppositions for the founding of a people, one that cannot take the place of any of the others, and in the absence of which the others count for nothing:

The folk *to whom the legislator is to give laws* must enjoy both peace and plenty. A state that is being founded is like a battalion that is being formed. This is the moment at which it is least capable of offering resistance, and *therefore* easiest to destroy; its people would offer more effective resistance in a period of complete disorder than in a time of fermentation *like this,* when each individual is concerned not about the danger *to the public thing* but about his own situation. Let a war or famine or revolt occur at this critical moment, and the state will be overthrown as a matter of course.

Not that we are without numerous examples of the establishment of governments during these stormy intervals. Such governments, however, themselves destroy the states in which they are established: usurpers invariably bring about, or seize upon, these periods of stress, so as to prevail upon the frightened people to approve destructive laws[26] that it would never adopt in a cool moment. The juncture chosen for the giving of laws is, *for this reason,* one of the surest marks by which to distinguish the handiwork of a legislator from that of a tyrant.

What *kind of* people is, on this showing, fit to receive laws? One which feels itself already tied together by some bond, whether of common origin or interest or agreement, but has not hitherto borne the yoke of genuine laws;[27] one which has no deeply-rooted customs or superstitions; one which has no fear of being overwhelmed by a sudden invasion; one which, while holding aloof from its neighbors' quarrels, is able either to defend itself unassisted against each of those neighbors, or to enlist the aid of the one in order to turn back the other; one in which it is possible for all the members to know one another; one which does not need to impose greater burdens on a man than he can bear; one which can get along without other peoples; one which other peoples can get along without; one which is neither rich nor poor, and is potentially self-sufficient; one, finally, which has the malleability of a young people and, along with it, the stability of an ancient people.

And I should like to add this to what I have said about doing without other peoples, and vice versa: Where two peoples live side by side, and one of them cannot get along without the other, you have a situation that is extremely difficult for the former and extremely dangerous for the latter. Any wise nation that finds itself in such a situation will promptly take energetic measures to free itself from its condition of dependency. The republic of Tlaxcala, an enclave in the Mexican empire, chose to live without salt rather than buy it—or even accept it as a gift—from the Mexicans. The knowing Tlaxcalans saw the trap concealed be-

neath the Mexicans' generosity, and remained free.
Nor is that all: this tiny state, completely sur-
rounded by a great empire, became in due time
the instrument of the latter's ruin.[28]

What renders the task of law-giving difficult
in many cases is not so much the need of calling
into existence *new* things as that of destroying *old*
things. And what makes successful law-giving rare
is the impossibility of finding the simplicity characteristic of nature in one and the same place with
the needs characteristic of society.

It is by no means easy to find a single people
that fulfills all the conditions I have named.[29] That
is why one sees few well-constituted states.

There is one European country that is still
capable of being legislated for, namely, the Island
of Corsica. Its gallant people, having shown so
much bravery and steadfastness in recovering and
defending its liberty, richly deserves to be taught,
by some wise man, how to preserve that liberty. I
have a feeling that this little island will one day
astonish Europe.

CHAPTER XI

Concerning the Different Systems of Laws

SUPPOSE we were to ask: the greatest of
all goods, the good that ought to be the goal of
every system of laws—of what precisely does it
consist?

It reduces itself, we should find, to two major elements, namely, liberty and equality: liberty, because any personal dependency represents just that amount of resources of which the body of the state is deprived; equality, because liberty cannot subsist without it.

I have already answered the question, What is liberty in civil society? As for equality, this word must not be understood to mean that all individuals must have exactly the same amount of power and wealth, but rather *(a)* that power must be exercised only in accordance with rank and the laws, so that no one shall have so much of it as to be able to use violence upon another,[30] and *(b)* that no citizen shall have so much wealth that he can buy another, and none so little that he is forced to sell himself. This presupposes moderation as regards both property and standing on the part of the great, and moderation as regards venality and covetousness on the part of the rank and file.

The way to give the state stability, then, is to narrow the distance between the extremes as much as possible, and tolerate neither paupers nor rich men. These two classes, which are inherently inseparable, are equally fatal to the common good. The one produces the fomenters of tyranny, the other the tyrants; and the traffic in civil liberty is always a deal between the former, who sell it, and the latter, who buy it.[31]

People say that the *kind* of equality I have just

defined is a *mere* speculative fancy, which is nowhere to be found in the real world. But does it
follow—from the fact that a bad state of affairs
is inevitable—that we should do nothing to counter-
act it? It is precisely because the pressure of
events always tends to destroy equality that the
pressure of the laws should always tend to preserve it.

These two broad purposes of every good system
of laws must be adapted, in each country, to the
relationships[32] arising out of the local situation
on the one hand and the character of the inhabitants on the other. And it is with an eye to these
relationships that we must prescribe for each people
the particular system of laws which, if not the best
in and of itself, is nevertheless the best for the state
for which it is intended. If, for example, your soil
is infertile and produces little, or if your territory
is too small for your population, turn your attention to industry and the mechanical arts; you will
be able to exchange their products for the food-
stuffs you require.

Do you live, rather, on land that is all fertile
plains and slopes? Is it a question of good land
and insufficient population? Then pour your
energies into agriculture, which breeds men, and
banish manufactures; the latter will herd your few
people together in towns, and will, in the long
run, merely depopulate your country. (As far as
the kingdom as a whole is concerned, writes M.
d'Argenson, the several branches of foreign trade

produce little or nothing over and above an illusory gain. They are capable of enriching a few individuals, even a few towns. But the nation as a whole has nothing to gain from them; nor are its people better off because of them.)[33]

Is your coastline long and easy of access? Then spread your ships over the entire ocean, and encourage commerce and navigation: your history will be brilliant—and brief. Are your sea-shores heaps of forbidding rocks? Then live on fish, and content yourselves with being barbarians: you will, as a result, live more tranquil lives—better lives perhaps, happier lives certainly.

In a word: leaving aside for a moment these principles applicable to all peoples, each people has in its make-up some element that gives the principles a particular application, and renders its system of laws just the right one for it to have. The Hebrews and the Arabs, the former long ago, the latter in recent times, took religion as their grand objective. The Athenians did as much with literature, the Carthaginians and the Tyrians with commerce, the Rhodesians with shipping, the Spartans with war, the Romans with virtue. The author of "The Spirit of the Laws" has shown by countless examples how the art of the legislator points systems of laws toward each of these objectives.

What gives genuine stability and long life to a state's constitution is this: the fact that it has fixed its attention upon what is called for, and in such fashion that the laws and the relations given by nature always operate in concert *and* upon the same points—the former merely emphasizing, going hand-in-hand with, or rectifying the latter. If, however, the state's legislator has seized upon the wrong objective, and has adopted some principle other than that which arises out of the nature of things—one making for servitude rather than one making for freedom, one making for riches rather than one making for large population, one making for peace rather than one making for conquests— the observable result will be a progressive but gradual weakening of the laws and a deterioration of the constitution. That state will be in constant turmoil until it has been destroyed or reformed, and the invincible forces of nature have reasserted their hegemony.

CHAPTER XII

Classification of the Laws

THERE are several relations that we must take into account if we are to bring order into the whole, *i.e.,* provide the best possible organization for the public thing.

There is, in the first place, the relation of the whole to the whole, or the sovereign to the state, *i.e.,* that which we observe when the body politic acts upon itself. This relation, as we shall see

below, can be resolved into relations among intermediate terms.[34]

The laws governing this relation are called
political laws, and are, not without reason where
they are wisely conceived, also called fundamental
laws. (*My position on this matter of fundamental
laws is as follows:* If there be one good way and
one only to order a given state, certainly its people, having once hit upon it, should cling to it.
But the order it has established may be bad; and
if so, what point is there in declaring fundamental
the very laws that prevent it from being good?
Nor is that all: A people, any way you look at it,
always has it within its power to change its laws,
including its best ones. For if it chooses to do itself
hurt, who is entitled to say it nay?)

There is, in the second place, the relation of the
state's individual members to one another and to
the body politic as a whole. This relation should
be minimized in the first of its two aspects and
maximized in the second: *i.e.,* each citizen should
be completely independent vis-à-vis each of the
others, and as dependent as can be vis-à-vis the
city.[35] This condition is invariably fulfilled in one
and the same way, the reason being that nothing
save the power of the state ever makes its individual members free. *Now:* The laws to which
this relation gives rise are called civil laws.

There is a third relation, this time between man
on the one hand and the law on the other,
namely the relation "disobedience: punishment."

It results in the promulgation of *what are called* criminal laws; *but* in the final analysis these are not so much a distinct type of law as the sanction for the other types.

There is, over and above the three types of law that we have already mentioned, a fourth, which is the most important of all. Laws of this type are engraved not upon tablets of marble or brass, but upon the hearts of the citizens. These laws it is that, acquiring new vigor with each passing day, make up the state's real constitution: When other laws become obsolescent or fall into desuetude, it is they that refurbish or replace them. It is they that keep a people within the spirit of its institutions, and gradually substitute the force of habit for the force of authority. I refer to the people's mores, to their customs, above all to their opinions, thus to an aspect *of the body politic* that our political theorists ignore—though the good health of its other aspects depends upon nothing else. This is, *accordingly,* the aspect over which the great legislator broods in secret. If he seems to confine his attention to particular enactments, these are *nevertheless* merely the arc of the arch, while the mores, which demand more patient midwifery, emerge finally as its unshakable keystone.

Of these several types of laws it is only the political, *i.e.,* those that determine the form of the government, that are relevant to my problem.

BOOK THREE

BEFORE discussing the various forms of government, let us try to assign a definite meaning to the word government; *for* I have not, up to this point, explained it very well.

CHAPTER I

Concerning Government in General

I WARN the reader that I have not mastered the art of making myself clear to the man who refuses to pay attention. The present chapter must be read carefully.

Every free action comes about through the concurrent operation of two causes. The first, which is the will that determines upon the action, we may call moral. The second, which is the force that performs the action, we may call physical. If I am to walk toward a certain object two things must happen: *(a)* I must will to go to it, and *(b)* my legs must carry me to it. The paralytic who wills to run is going to remain where he is; but so also is the fleet-footed man who does not will to run.

The same two causes operate *to produce free actions* in a political society. Here also we can perceive a distinction between will, which we meet under the name of the legislative power, and force, which we meet under the name of the executive power. Nothing is or should be done in a political society without their concurrence.

The legislative power belongs—must belong—to the people, and the people only; so much I have already demonstrated. The executive power, by contrast, cannot belong to the collectivity qua law-making or sovereign body; that is a conclusion easily arrived at by reasoning—*in the following manner*—from other principles I have advanced: The executive power is concerned exclusively with particular acts; the latter lie entirely outside the province of the law; the sovereign acts exclusively through laws; particular acts, *and by the same token the executive power itself,* are therefore completely beyond the sovereign's competence.

All this points up the need for a special agency *whose responsibility it would be:* to marshal the energies of the body politic, and set them to work as the general will may direct; to serve as a means of communication between the state and the sovereign; and to accomplish within the collective person, in a manner of speaking, that which the link between body and soul accomplishes within the individual man. We need, then, look no further for the reason for having a government in the state. It is, however, merely the sovereign's agent. To confuse it with the sovereign is to fall into error.

What then is the government? *I define it as follows:* A body that has been created to maintain communication between subjects and sovereign, and that, *accordingly,* occupies an intermediate position between them. It is charged with *(a)* the execution of the laws, and *(b)* the preservation of both civil and political liberty.

The several members of this body are called officials or kings—or, what amounts to the same thing, rulers, and the body as a whole is called the prince. (Thus the Venetians, even when their Doge is absent, address their collegial executive as "Most Serene Prince.")[1]

Those authors are clearly in the right, then, who argue that the act by which a people places itself under rulers is not in any sense a contract: it is purely and simply a grant of a commission— or, *if you like,* an employment. The rulers, in performing the duties attaching to this employment, are—*I repeat*—mere agents of the sovereign: they exercise, in the latter's name, precisely the amount of power it has placed in their hands. Nor is that all: The actual alienation of that power *by the sovereign* would be contrary to the purpose for which the association was formed, and irreconcilable with the nature of political society. Thus the sovereign is entitled to limit or modify or revoke the power it places in their hands when and as it sees fit.

I shall, then, use the term government, or supreme administration, to denote the legitimate exercise of executive power, and the term prince, or magistrate, to refer to the man or body of men responsible for the said supreme administration.

It is within the government that we can observe the intermediate forces whose reciprocal relations, taken together, constitute the relation of all to all, that is, of the sovereign to the state. This relation can be conceived as that between the extreme terms of a continuous proportion, in which the mean proportional is the government (which receives from the sovereign the orders it gives to the people). And *I hold that* the state can be on an even keel only when, all things considered, the power (or action) of the government is equal to the power (or action) of the citizens—the latter being the sovereign in one of their capacities and the subjects in another.

It is, I hold further, impossible to cause any one of the three terms of our continuous proportion to vary without instantly destroying its proportionality. If for example the sovereign attempts to govern, or if the prince attempts to hand down laws, or if the subjects refuse to obey, order gives way to confusion: will and force cease to act in concert; the state, already dissolved *to all intents and purposes,* sinks either into despotism or into anarchy. In a word: There is only one mean proportional possible for any given pair of extreme terms; and there is, in the same way, only one right form of government possible for any given state. (This right form of government is not, however, one and the same for different peoples, or even for one and the same people at different times. The reason for this is that any one of countless events is capable of modifying the relations that obtain within a people.)

In an attempt to convey some idea of the various relations that may obtain between our two extreme terms, I shall now take as an example the number of citizens, which provides a comparatively easy relation to explain.

Let us suppose a state with 10,000 citizens. The sovereign can be regarded—*as we have seen above* —only collectively, that is, as a body, while with the citizens qua subjects *it is quite otherwise:* we regard each of them as an individual. In the situation we are assuming, then, the sovereign is to the subject as 10,000 is to 1; which is to say that each member of the state is wholly subordinated to the sovereign authority, but enjoys, as his share, only one ten-thousandth of that authority.

If now we suppose the people to number, 100,000 *instead of only 10,000,* we find the status of the individual members qua subjects unchanged: each of them, just as before, bears the full weight of the laws. But the vote each of them casts is now reduced to a hundred-thousandth of the total, with the result that each vote exerts only one-tenth of its former influence upon the shaping of those laws. Now: since the subject has a constant value *for this purpose* of 1, the ratio "sovereign : subjects" *necessarily* increases in proportion as the number of citizens increases. And from this it follows that each increase in the state's numbers means a *proportionate* reduction in the amount of liberty.

When I say that the ratio *"sovereign : subjects"* increases, I understand this to mean that it moves further and further away from equality. In other words, the greater the ratio in the geometrician's sense of the term the smaller it is in the sense of the term as used by the ordinary man—*who describes things as "out of all proportion to one another" when they differ greatly*. In the first case the proportion is conceived in quantitative terms, and is measured by a quotient; in the second case it is conceived in terms of degree of similarity, and varies inversely with the width of the gap.

Now: the smaller the similarity between the several individual wills and the general will, which is to say between the mores and the laws, the more repressive force must be augmented. As the number of citizens increases, therefore, the government must, in order to be the right government, be relatively stronger.

Any increment in the size of the state, however, places the depositaries of public authority under an increased temptation to abuse it, and simultaneously provides them with increased facilities for doing so. And since that is true, the greater the power the government needs to contain the people, the greater the power the sovereign needs, in its turn, to contain the government. I do not speak here of power in absolute terms, but rather of the relative power of the several parts of the state.

It follows from the foregoing dual relationship that the continuous proportion "sovereign : prince : people" is not an arbitrary concept by any means: it is, rather, an unavoidable inference from the nature of political society. This follows too: since one of the *proportion's* two extreme terms, namely, the people regarded as subjects, is a constant represented by the number 1, whenever the doubled proportion increases or diminishes the simple proportion increases or diminishes in like manner— with the result that the mean proportional changes. All of which goes to show that there is no single way of constituting a government that is mandatory in all cases—that, on the contrary, there can be as many governments of different character as there are states of different size.

If someone, by way of caricaturing this method of explaining the matter, were to accuse me of thinking that all you have to do—in order to arrive at the mean proportional and determine the shape of the government—is extract the square root of the number representing the population, my answer would run as follows: I use the population figure here merely as an example, inasmuch as the relations I have in mind are to be measured in terms not of the population alone, but of the overall quantity of action, which depends upon a great multitude of factors. If, for the rest, I borrow certain terms from geometry, in order to express myself in fewer words, I am well aware that the precision characteristic of geometry cannot be reproduced in *propositions concerning* moral quantities.

What political society is on a large scale, government within political society is on a small one: a moral person endowed with certain faculties, now active like the sovereign, now passive like the state, and—like political society once again—capable of being broken down into a network of relations. The latter, as we should expect, gives us a further continuous proportion, and within it still another, reflecting the position of the several agencies of the government, so that we arrive finally at an indivisible mean proportional, *i.e.,* a single ruler, or supreme magistrate, of whom we may think as the numeral 1, situated in the middle of the series at which we have arrived, with fractions lined up on one side and whole numbers on the other.

Lest we bog down in this morass of terms, let us now be content to regard the government as a body within the state—one that is additional to and distinct from the people on the one hand and the sovereign on the other, and that serves as a connecting link between them.

There is this essential difference between the
state and the government: The former owes its
existence to nothing outside of or other than itself;
the latter exists only by command of the sovereign.
The prince, accordingly, has or should have no
guiding will except the general will, or the law,
and no powers other than those vested in it by
public action. The moment it attempts to spin out
of itself any autonomous or independent action,
the connectedness of the larger body begins to be
impaired. Let the time ever come, moreover, when
the prince's private will has become more vigorous
than the will of the sovereign, let the time ever
come when the prince is turning the powers lodged
in it to purposes dictated by that private will, let
the time ever come when, in consequence, there
are, so to speak, two sovereigns, one de jure and
another de facto—let all that happen, and the social
bond will instantly disappear, and the body politic
disintegrate.

If, on the other hand, the government is to have
a real life and being, to keep it distinct from the
body of the state, if its members are to act in
concert, and forward the purpose for which it has
been established, it needs *to develop* its own moral
self: its sensibility, common to all of its members;
its own internal sources of strength; its own will
concerned with its own preservation. All this presupposes assemblies and councils, with the power
to deliberate and make decisions. It further presupposes rights and titles and privileges belonging

exclusively to the prince—of such character that the greater the burdens an official carries the greater the honors he receives.

The problem is this: How organize this subordinate whole within the broader one so as to keep it from strengthening its own constitution at the expense of the state's? How organize it so that it shall never fail to distinguish between its private *or corporate* power, *which is developed within itself and is* intended for its preservation, and its public power, *which is conveyed to it by the sovereign and is* intended for the preservation of the state? How organize it, finally, so that it shall always stand ready to sacrifice the government to the people rather than the people to the government?

One further point: The government is, to be sure, an artificial body created by another artificial body; in a sense *therefore* its very existence is a borrowed and subordinate existence. Even so, *it is like other living things in that* it moves with greater or lesser vigor and speed, and—if I may put it so—enjoys a greater or lesser degree of robust health. Nor is that all: it is capable, without actually turning its back upon the purpose for which it was established, of deviating from that purpose to a greater or lesser extent, according as it is *well or ill* constituted.

Because of the wide range of possibilities *suggested* in the preceding paragraph, there are many correct relationships between the government and the main body of the state, *rather than a single one—each* depending upon the relations, contingent and private in character, by which the state itself is always being transformed. For unless its relationships are continuously modified, and in a way that takes into account the shortcomings of the body politic to which it belongs, that government which is best in and of itself will often degenerate into the worst.

CHAPTER II

Concerning the Constituting Principle of the Several Forms of Government

As A FIRST step toward setting forth a general theory to explain the wide range of possibilities I have just mentioned, we must now draw a distinction—parallel to that which we have drawn between state and sovereign—between prince and rulers.[2]

A governing body can have a greater or lesser number of members, *just as a political society can have a greater or lesser number of citizens. Now:* I have already shown how, *in political society,* the proportion "sovereign : subjects" varies directly with the number of citizens. And we can, by availing ourselves of an obvious analogy, lay down a similar proposition[3] about the proportion "government : officials."

The total power of the government, because invariably equal to the total power of the state, is itself invariable. The more of its power it expends upon its own members, therefore, the less it has left with which to act upon the entire people.

It follows from the above that a government grows weaker as the number of officials increases. Since this principle is basic, let us try to make it quite clear.

We can distinguish, within the personality of each official, three wills, each essentially different from the other two: *(a)* his will as an individual; *(b)* a will that he wills in common with all the officials; and *(c)* the will of the people or, if you like, of the sovereign. The first of the three looks exclusively to his private advantage. The second, which looks exclusively to the advantage of the prince, might well be called the corporate will of the government: while it is a general will from the standpoint of the government, it is merely a particular will from the standpoint of the state of which the government is a part. The third is general from both standpoints—that of the state regarded as a whole and that of the government regarded as a part of the whole.

In *a state with* a perfect set of laws, the private or individual will would be inoperative, the corporate will of the government in a decidedly subordinate position, and the general or sovereign will, consequently, in continuous command of the entire scene—*i.e.,* in continuous service as the exclusive guiding principle for the other two.

Wherever nature is having its way, on the other hand, each of the three wills makes itself felt just to the extent that it is concentrated. Everywhere we turn, therefore, we find the general will the weakest of the three—*i.e., occupying the lowest rung on the ladder,* with the corporate will of the government occupying the second rung and the private will the first rung. In a word: each member of the government is himself first, an official second, and a citizen third—thus reversing the order that *healthy* social organization calls for.

We can, with all that in mind, readily see this: where a single individual has the entire government in his hands, private will and corporate will are entirely at one, and the latter is accordingly at its highest possible peak of intensity. Now: The absolute amount of the government's power is, as we have seen, invariable. But the extent to which power is actually used depends *always* upon the degree of intensity of the will *that is directing it.* The most vigorous of governments, therefore, is a government of one man.

Where, on the other hand, government and legislative authority are in the same hands, *i.e.,* where the sovereign itself is prince and every last citizen an official, what happens is this: The corporate will and the general will converge, the former has as little vigor as the latter, and private will remains as strong as ever. The relative power and vigor of the government—its absolute power, let us remember, is always the same—are accordingly at their lowest point.

The foregoing incontestable relationships are further confirmed by certain other considerations, as follows:

In the first place, each official is evidently more active within the body to which he belongs than each citizen within that to which he belongs. The government's actions are accordingly influenced by the private wills *of its members* much more than the sovereign's by those of its members—if only because the official is almost always individually responsible for some specific function of government, while the citizen is not individually responsible for any specific function of sovereignty.

Secondly, the power of the state increases in absolute amount as the state itself expands—the former's rate of increase lagging, to be sure, behind the latter's rate of expansion. The officials, by contrast, increase their numbers—assuming *for the moment* a state whose magnitude is given—in vain: the government does not acquire, in consequence of the added numbers, a larger absolute amount of power, because its power is at all times equal to that of the state, and the amount of the state's power is invariable. The government's relative power or vigor accordingly diminishes *as the number of its members increases,* while any absolute increase in its power remains out of the question.

Thirdly, business undeniably gets itself dispatched more slowly as the number of persons responsible for it increases: They become excessively cautious, and take too few chances; often, as they are busy deliberating, they let the moment of opportunity slip past—with the result that the fruits of deliberation are lost.

I have just proved that the government becomes less and less effective as the number of officials increases—just as, in an earlier section, I showed that repressive force must be applied on an ever larger scale as the population increases. It follows from the two propositions together that the proportion "officials : government" should vary inversely with the proportion "subjects : sovereign," which is to say: the more the population increases the more the government should be compressed. The number of officials, in other words, should be reduced with, and in proportion to, every increase in population.

I am speaking here, be it noted, not of the government's legitimacy but of its power, and in relative terms *at that.* For as the number of officials increases, the corporate will *of the government* moves closer and closer, in point of fact, to the general will, *and vice versa:* if there is a single magistrate the corporate will, as I was saying a moment ago, is merely a private will. Any gain in the one direction (*i.e., legitimacy*) is thus accompanied by a loss in the other (*i.e., power*). The skill of the legislator accordingly consists in

knowing how to determine the point at which the
will and the power of the government, which
as far as the former's legitimacy is concerned vary
inversely, are brought into that relation with one
another that is most advantageous to the state.

CHAPTER III

Concerning the Classification of Governments

WE HAVE SEEN in the preceding chapter
why the various types or forms of government are
classified according to number of members. In
this chapter we have the further task of considering how they are classified.

1) The sovereign can put the government in
the hands of the entire people, or the largest
fraction thereof, in such fashion that the number
of citizen-officials will exceed the number of plain
private citizens. The term applied to this form
of government is "democracy."

2) The sovereign can, rather, compress the
government within the hands of a small number
of persons, so that there will be more plain citizens
than officials. The name applied to this form of
government is "aristocracy."

3) The sovereign can concentrate the entire
government in the hands of a single official, from
whom *all* other officials will hold the power they
exercise. The name applied to this form of govern-

ment, the commonest of all, is "monarchy," or "royal government."

It should be noticed that all three of these forms, or at least the first two, are—over a considerable latitude—matters of more or less. A democracy, for example, can embrace all the people, or be confined to only half of them. An aristocracy, in turn, may include at one extreme an indeterminately small fraction of the people and at the other extreme as many as half of them. Even royal government, for that matter, can be shared to some extent: Sparta always had two kings, that being the number required by its constitution, and the Roman Empire sometimes had as many as eight emperors—without anyone's being able to say that the empire itself had been divided. At some point, in a word, each form of government begins to shade into the next in the series. And, while we have only the three *basic* classifications, we readily perceive that the number of alternative forms of government is, in strict accuracy, always equal to the number of the state's citizens.

Nor is that all: a given government can for certain purposes be divided into various parts, one of which is administered in one way and another in another. This means that the three forms can, by being combined in various ways, give rise to a wide variety of mixed forms, each of which we may multiply by the number of simple forms (*i.e., by three*).

Men have vigorously debated the question "What

is the best form of government?" from the earliest times. In doing so they have overlooked the fact that each of the forms is now the best and now the worst, according to the circumstances.

If the number of supreme magistrates should *indeed* vary inversely with the number of citizens, we may infer that, in general, democracy is the form of government appropriate to small states, aristocracy that appropriate to states of middling size, and monarchy that appropriate to large states.

The rule follows as a matter of course from the principle *I have advanced*. But who is to list the many special circumstances that might provide exceptions to it?

CHAPTER IV

Concerning Democracy

NOBODY knows so well as the law-maker himself how the law should be executed and interpreted. It would seem, therefore, that the best possible constitution would be one lodging the executive and legislative powers in the same hands. A government exercising both these powers is nevertheless ipso facto inadequate on some counts. For under such a government things that ought to be treated differently are not so treated: prince and sovereign, here one and the same *moral* person, constitute so to speak a government without a government.

A fuller statement of the objections to such a constitution might well run as follows:

It is never healthy for the maker of laws to execute them, or for the people as a body to withdraw its attention from matters of general interest and fix it upon particular objects. Nothing can be more dangerous than the impact of private interests upon public affairs, so that *if we must choose* between the government's abusing the laws and the legislator's being corrupted (which is what invariably happens when private matters are brought within its purview), the former evil is the lesser one. For the state whose legislator is corrupted degenerates in the very fibre of its being, with the result that reform of any kind ceases to be possible. A people that would never misuse the power of government, *on the other hand,* would never misuse independence either; *which is to say that* one that would govern well at all times would at no time need to be governed.

No real democracy—taking this term in its most rigorous sense—ever existed, and none ever will exist. For the many to govern and the few to be governed is to go against natural order. *Nor is that all:* A people constantly assembled to dispatch public business is impossible to imagine; nor, evidently, can any people possibly set up agencies for that purpose without thereby bringing about a change in its form of government.

In a word, I think it safe to advance the following principle: when the functions of government are shared out among several agencies, the smaller ones win for themselves, sooner or later, supreme power—if only because of the ease with which they dispatch business, this being a natural avenue to power.

For the rest, how many things that are difficult to bring together in one and the same place this form of government presupposes! *You must have:*

a) A very small state, in which the people can easily be assembled, and each citizen can—without going to much trouble—get acquainted with all the others.

b) Great simplicity of mores, which cuts down both the volume of business and the number of thorny discussions.

c) A high degree of equality as regards rank and fortune, without which it is impossible for equal rights and equal authority to last very long.

And, finally, *d)* either no luxury at all, or very little. For luxury either results from riches or renders riches necessary: It corrupts the rich by making them possessive and the poor by making them covetous. It puts the country up for sale, whether to indulgence or to vanity. It robs the state of all its citizens—to make some the slaves of others and each the slave of *public* opinion.

A celebrated author has named virtue as the guiding principle appropriate to republics. The above considerations show why: in the absence of virtue the conditions we have enumerated could not conceivably continue to be fulfilled. But this same brilliant genius, having failed to draw all the necessary distinctions, often thought in a slip-shod manner, and was sometimes not very clear-headed. He therefore missed the following point: Since the sovereign authority is everywhere the same, the same principle *he was advancing* should be valid for every well-constituted state—though to a greater or lesser degree according as it has this form of government or that one.

One additional point: democratic or popular government is more subject than any other to civil wars and *other* internal disturbances—in part because of its stronger and more persistent tendency to change into another form, in part because of the greater vigilance and courage it requires for its maintenance. It, beyond all others, is the constitutional form under which the citizen must arm himself with both might and constancy—and must, each day, echo in the depths of his heart the words the virtuous Paladin of Posnonia—a Duke of Lorraine who sired a king of Poland[4]—once uttered in the Polish Diet: "Better liberty with danger than peace with slavery."[5]

While a people made up of gods, if one were to exist, would govern itself democratically, no such perfect form of government is advisable for one made up of mere men.

CHAPTER V

Concerning Aristocracy

IN THE present chapter, *unlike the last,* we have to do with two distinct moral persons, government and sovereign, and thus two general wills, one general with respect to all the citizens, the other general with respect only to the members of the administration. (This type of government can, therefore, address itself to the subjects only as the agent of the sovereign, *i.e.,* the people itself, though in arranging its internal affairs it may act as it sees fit. That we must bear constantly in mind.)

The earliest societies all governed themselves aristocratically: the heads of families met from time to time to make decisions about public affairs, and young folk subordinated themselves without question to the authority of experience. Thus the terms "priests," "elders," "senate," "gerontocracy." That is how the savages of South America govern themselves even today. And they are very well governed indeed.

As, however, man-made inequality triumphed with the passing of time over natural inequality —*for* the ancients' word "optimates" clearly means "most powerful" rather than "best" [6]—, wealth and power came to be more highly esteemed than age. Aristocracies *therefore* became elective. And in the end, what with the handing down of power plus property from father to offspring, the latter's families acquired patrician status, government became hereditary, and men twenty years old occupied seats in senates.

We can, in view of the foregoing, distinguish three types of aristocracy: the natural, the elective, and the hereditary. The first of these is inadvisable for any save simple peoples. The third is the worst possible form of government. The second, aristocracy in its strict sense, is the best possible form of government.

Aristocratic government makes a distinction, *which we have seen to be desirable,* between the two powers, and has the further advantage that attaches to a selected membership. Under a popular government, citizens become officials merely by getting themselves born; under this type of government only a limited number of them become officials at all, and these only by election. Probity, vision, experience, along with all the other qualities that public preference and public esteem take into account, accordingly become so many further guarantees that the society shall be wisely governed. (The procedures by which officials are elected must, however, be provided by law, and for the following reason: The government, where this matter is left to the discretion of the prince, degenerates inevitably into hereditary aristocracy —which is what happened both in the republic of Venice and in that of Berne. The first of these, to be sure, long ago reached the moment of its dissolution as a state; and if the second has been kept alive, that is only because of the unequaled sagacity of its senate. It is an honorable but decidedly dangerous exception.)[7]

Secondly, *aristocracy has these advantages over democracy:* assemblies are easier to convene; business is discussed more fully, and dispatched in a more orderly and diligent manner. And the good reputation of the state abroad, here in the hands of venerable senators, is safer than it would be in those of an anonymous, or even despised, multitude.

For the wise to govern the many is, in a word, both the best and the most natural way of ordering things—where you can be certain that they will govern not in their own interest but in the interest of the many. The useless multiplication of instrumentalities is absolutely indefensible; so is the employment of twenty thousand men on a task that a hundred men chosen for the purpose can do better.

We must notice, however, that under this form of government corporate interest begins, at some point, to direct collective energies less and less into the channels authorized by the general will. We must notice, too, that aristocracy has an inherent tendency, not mentioned above, which withholds a part of the executive power from *its task of executing* the law.

Let us turn now to requirements of a more

specific character: Aristocracy requires that the state not be so small, or the people so simple and upright, that execution of the laws follows as a matter of course upon the declaration of the general will—as it does in a healthy democracy. It further requires that the state not be so large that the officials, scattered about over the country to govern it, can cut themselves off—each in his own department—from the sovereign and, as a first step toward becoming overlords, make themselves independent.

But if aristocracy demands less in the way of virtues than popular government, it does call for certain virtues peculiar to itself. Among them— since rigorous equality would seem out of place here, and did not obtain even in Sparta—are moderation on the part of the rich and contentment on the part of the poor.

On the other hand, while this form of government certainly involves some inequality of wealth, the latter's function is that of confiding administration, in general, to those who with least inconvenience can devote full time to it—and by no means, as Aristotle would have us believe, that of causing the rich always to be preferred. On the contrary: it is of the first importance that the people, by occasionally electing men who are not wealthy, should learn that merit affords more compelling grounds for preference than wealth.

CHAPTER VI

Concerning Monarchy

IN THE foregoing chapters we have been thinking of a collective prince, *i.e.,* of the state's executive power as lodged in a *moral* person held together by the operation of the laws. We must now think of that power as concentrated in the hands of a flesh-and-blood individual—a natural person—with an exclusive right to exercise it in conformity with the laws. To such a man we apply the term "monarch," or "king."

In the other forms of government we have a collective being acting as an individual. Here, by sharp contrast, we have an individual acting as a collective being: the prince's moral identity is thus a physical identity as well. In it we find, in natural combination, the several elements which, under other forms of government, the law must strive so hard to bring together.

Everything, then—the will of the people, the will of the prince, the public power of the state, the corporate strength of the government—is geared under this form to one and the same prime mover. Every wheel of the machine is controlled by one and the same hand. Everything works on behalf of one and the same objective. There is no question of motions that are at cross-purposes with one another, and so cancel one another out. Under no other type of constitution conceivable can action on so large a scale be produced with so little effort. I think of Archimedes—seated quietly on the bank as he effortlessly draws a huge ship along the water's surface—as the symbol of the able monarch: apparently without himself lifting a finger, he keeps everything moving, and thus, never budging from his cabinet, governs his vast domains.

There is, then, no form of government that possesses greater vigor. But there is also none in which private will operates more powerfully, or gains the upper hand with less difficulty. Everything, certainly, works toward one and the same objective. But that objective is not by any means the happiness of the people—*which means that* this vigorous form of government continually produces —in direct proportion to its own vigor—results prejudicial to the state.

All monarchs try to become absolute monarchs, and there are persons who are forever crying out to them from far places that their best means to that end is to get themselves loved by their peoples. A fine maxim this, and not entirely wide of the mark. Alas, however, the day will never come when it has ceased to be ridiculed at court. The power that accrues to a monarch from the love of his people is the greatest power he can have? No doubt. But it is power of a precarious kind: one holds it on terms, and no prince will ever content himself with it. Even the best of kings wish to be free to do wicked things whenever they like, and still keep on being kings. When, *therefore,* some political sermonizer tells them that the monarch's strength is one and the same thing with that of his people—that his primary concern is, accordingly, a flourishing, numerous, and formidable people—it is sheer waste of breath. They know better. Their primary concern, as individuals, is for their peoples to be weak and miserable—*i.e.,* incapable at all times of offering any resistance. If we could take for granted complete and sustained submissiveness on the part of the subjects, then indeed it would be in the prince's interest for his people to become strong—in order that their strength, which on this showing would be one and the same thing with his own, might give him stature in the eyes of his neighbors. In actual fact, however, the prince's interest in the people's strength is at most secondary and subordinate, which is to say that the two suppositions (*the people are powerful, and their strength is one and the same with his own*) are incompatible. Quite naturally, therefore, princes give their preference to the more immediately useful of the two maxims.

That is the point that Samuel strongly urged upon the Hebrews. It is also the point that Machiavelli made crystal-clear: He pretended to instruct kings, but was really giving lessons—important lessons furthermore—to their peoples, so that his "Prince" is, for republicans, the book of books.

Machiavelli was an upright man, and a good citizen. Because of his tie to the house of Medici, however, no course was open to him—given the oppressive régime in his country—save to disguise his love of liberty. The very fact that he chose so execrable a protagonist as Caesar Borgia lays his secret intention sufficiently bare; and the clash between the principles of his book "The Prince" and those of his "Discourses on Livy" and "History of Florence" is proof that up to the present moment this profound political theorist has been read only by the superficial or the corrupt. The Vatican has placed a severe ban on his book. No wonder! That is the court he depicts most faithfully.[8]

We have already seen, in canvassing the broad relationships *among prince, sovereign, and people,* that monarchy is suitable only to large states; nor do we reach a different conclusion if we examine monarchy in terms of its own distinctive characteristics. The more numerous the public administrators, the smaller the difference between the prince and the subjects, and the greater the approximation to equality, so that in *e.g.* a democracy prince and subjects are as one to one—*i.e.,* there is complete equality. This difference increases as the government becomes more restricted, and is at its maximum when executive power is vested in one man. What happens then is this: the distance between prince and people being excessive, adequate coordination *of the parts* within the state is out of the question, and can be provided only by orders occupying intermediate positions between them—along with princelings and grandees and nobles to fill their ranks. That kind of thing, however, is bad for a small state, where so many distinctions in rank invariably spell ruin.

On the other hand, if—*as we have seen*—it is difficult for a large state ever to be well-governed, for such a state to be well-governed by one man is very difficult indeed. And everyone knows what happens when the king surrounds himself with deputies.

One inherent and unavoidable shortcoming of monarchical government—one because of which it will always stand well below republican government *in the scale of excellence*—we may put as follows: Under republican forms of government, public opinion almost never elevates to important posts any save enlightened and capable men, who subsequently fill them with great distinction. The men who succeed under monarchical forms of government, on the other hand, are usually mischief-makers, cheats, intriguers—and petty ones at that: once they are in high office, the meager talents that have won them preferment at court merely enable them to make a public display of their incompetence. Peoples go wrong much less often than princes when it comes to choosing high officials: a man of genuine merit in a *king's* ministry is, indeed, a spectacle almost as rare as a nincompoop at the head of a republican government. And when—in some monarchy well-nigh undone by successive sets of these petty stewards and bailiffs—a happy accident brings to the direction of affairs a man born to govern, the resources on which he is able to lay his hands evoke astonishment on all sides; his advent to power marks a turning-point in his country's history.

In order for a monarchical state to be well-governed, its magnitude, *i.e.,* its territorial extension, would have to vary with the capacities of the man called upon to govern it. Conquering *territories* is much easier than governing *them:* provide a man a long enough lever, and he will give the world a jolt by merely wiggling his fingers—but only a Hercules can bear its weight right on his shoulders. As for the small state, no matter how small it is, its prince is almost invariably too small for it; and in those rare cases where it is the other way 'round, *i.e.,* where the state is too small for its prince, it is still badly governed, for the following reason: The prince, by constantly following the path prescribed by the broad sweep of his designs, forgets the interests of his people; such a prince will, indeed, make his people as unhappy by misusing his over-supply of talents as ever a more dull-witted ruler will make them by having too few. Thus the truly desirable state of affairs would be one—if I may put it so—in which the state, at the beginning of each reign, expanded or contracted its frontiers to fit the capacities of its new prince. *To which we must add this:* Since the talents of a senate, by contrast, vary within relatively narrow limits, the state that has one can maintain constant boundaries without hurt to its administration.

The most conspicuous disadvantage of a government of one man is that it does not provide that regularized succession which, under the other two forms, assures uninterrupted continuity. When the king dies you must get another king: *if you elect him,* there are dangerous intervals for the holding of elections—besides which the elections themselves are stormy affairs which, save as the citizens possess a kind of disinterestedness and integrity that are unusual under this form, are *likely to be* tainted with bribery and corruption. *Nor is that all:* The chances are that the man to whom the state has sold itself will resell it in due time, and recoup out of the pockets of the weak the sums extorted from him by the powerful. Soon or late, under such a government, everything becomes venal, and once this has happened, the peace men enjoy when a king is on the throne is *even* less tolerable than the disorder of the interregna.

What steps have people taken to forestall these evils? They have declared crowns hereditary within certain families. They have legislated succession acts, to prevent disputes of any kind upon the death of the king—*i.e.,* they have exchanged the disadvantages of elections for those of regencies, and so opted for surface tranquillity in preference to wise government. They have, that is to say, preferred the risk of having children and monsters and imbeciles as rulers to contests over the election of good kings. What they have failed to take into account is this: when you expose yourself to this horn of the dilemma you play a game in which your chances of winning are well-nigh nil. Young Dionysius' reply to his father—who had reproached him for a shameful action by asking, "Did I set you the example?"—hit the nail right on the head: "Ah! *But* your father was not a king."

Everything conspires to steal away the reason and justice of the man brought up to command others. Great pains are taken—so at least we are told—to teach young princes the art of reigning. A better plan—since none of these pains seems to do them any good—would be to start them out on lessons in the art of obeying. History's greatest kings were not reared to occupy a throne at all: the science of kingship is, *indeed,* one that no one has mastered so little as the man who has learned too much about it, and also one that a man masters sooner by obeying orders than by giving them. "The best and quickest means of distinguishing between good and evil is this: ask yourself what you would and what you would not have willed— had someone else been king." [9] (From Tacitus' "Histories.") [10]

One consequence of the discontinuity to which I referred a moment ago is instability: Royal government bases itself first on one plan then on another—according as the ruling prince or the men who rule for him are of this character or that. It therefore cannot, over any considerable period, preserve either a fixed objective or a consistent pattern of conduct. Such inconstancy—resulting, as it does, in the state's drifting from policy-maxim to policy-maxim and from project to project—is to be found in neither of the other forms of government, where the prince is never replaced—so that if courts show more cunning than senates, senates usually show more sagacity than courts. Republics move toward their objectives along lines of policy that are not only more stable *than those of a king's ministry,* but also more capably pursued. For every shake-up in the king's ministry—since all ministers and most kings follow the rule: handle all problems by doing the opposite of what your predecessor did—produces a shake-up in the state itself.

The instability characteristic of royal government offers us the means of dealing with a trick argument frequently employed by royalist political theorists. These theorists not only liken civil government to domestic government, and thus the prince to the father of a family (a fallacy that we have already disposed of); they also, with great liberality, endow the prince with every virtue that he might conceivably need. *In short:* They take it for granted that the prince is invariably what he ought to be. On such a showing royal government is evidently preferable to any other possible form:

undeniably the strongest of governments, it would likewise be the best of governments if its corporate will were not so likely to be at odds with the general will.

If, however, as Plato assures us in his "Politicus" [11] "kings by nature" are a scarce breed, how often will nature and fortune join forces—and place a crown on one's head? If royal upbringing necessarily corrupts those who receive it, what are we entitled to expect from a succession of men brought up to occupy the throne? To identify royal government with government by a good king is, in a word, to practice self-deception: anyone who wishes to see this type of government as it really is must observe it *not only at its best, but also* under princes who are stupid or wicked—as they will be when they ascend the throne, or will become as a result of sitting on it.

Although the authors we read are not unaware of these problems, they are not bothered by them in the least. The proper course, they assure us, is to obey—and keep a civil tongue in our heads. Bad kings are inflicted upon us by an angry God: our lot is to accept them with good grace as punishments sent from heaven—an edifying line of argument, no doubt, but one that would perhaps feel more at home in a pulpit than in a treatise on politics. What would we say of a doctor who promised miracles, but whose entire skill lay in urging his patient to be long-suffering? We know

all too well that we must put up with a bad
government—when a bad government is what we
have. The trick we need to learn is how to invent
a good one.

CHAPTER VII

Concerning Mixed Government

THERE IS, strictly speaking, no such thing
as a government simple in form. A single ruler
must have his subordinate officials; a popular
government must have its head man. The sharing
out of executive power is thus always a matter of
degree—of a larger number *of officials* or a lesser.

We may, however, draw the following distinction: in some cases the larger number depends
upon the lesser, in others the lesser upon the
larger. *In still other cases neither depends on the
other.* The executive power, *that is to say,* is sometimes shared out equally, whether because—as
with the government of England—the constituent
parts are mutually dependent, or because—as in
Poland—each of the constituent parts exercises an
authority which, though fragmentary, is nevertheless independent. The second *(i.e., Polish)* arrange-
ment is unsatisfactory: *it results in a* government
that lacks unity and a state that is insufficiently
coordinated.

Which is preferable—one of the simple forms of government, or a mixed government? To this question, with which political theorists have preoccupied themselves a great deal, our answer is necessarily the same as our answer concerning forms of government in general.

A simple form of government—precisely because of its simplicity—is preferable, in and of itself, to any other. But in any state in which the executive power is insufficiently dependent on the sovereign, in which, that is to say, the proportion "prince : sovereign" exceeds the proportion "people : prince," the imbalance must be corrected by dividing the government. Each of the several parts will then exercise undiminished authority over the subjects, while the fact of its being divided will make the administration as a whole less powerful vis-à-vis the sovereign.

Another means of coping with this same problem is to create intermediate officials whose task it would be—without so much as touching the government—to maintain equilibrium between the two powers, and preserve their respective rights. This, however, would be a moderated form of government, not a mixed form.

Measures of this general type can also be used wherever the opposite kind of imbalance occurs—*i.e.,* agencies can be created to pull together a government that is not vigorous enough. All democracies employ this device. You divide the government in the one case to make it weaker, in the other to make it stronger. The extremes—both strength and weakness—are associated with the simple forms of government, and the middle ground, in between the extremes, with the mixed forms.

CHAPTER VIII

Each Form of Government Not Appropriate to Just Any Country

LIBERTY is not one of those fruits that thrive in just any climate. It is not, therefore, to be plucked by just any people.

The more you meditate about this principle— it was first advanced by Montesquieu—the more convinced you become of its validity. And the more you exert yourself to refute it, the more ground you open up for new arguments in support of it.

The public person, under all forms of government the world has ever seen, consumes without producing. From what source then does it draw what it consumes? From labor on the part of its individual members. Public needs, *that is to say,* are provided for out of the surpluses of individuals. And from this it follows that the civil state can exist only where men's labor yields something over and above what they themselves need.

Now: the various countries of the world do not all produce the required surplus in one and the same amount. In a goodly number of countries it is large, in others middling, in others zero, in yet others less than zero—depending on the fertility of the region, the kind of labor the land calls for, the nature of what is produced, the vigor of the inhabitants and the level of consumption they require, and certain other quantities, of this general character, that must be taken into account.

Governments themselves, for the rest, are not all alike. They are, *for example,* more or less voracious —the more and less depending, in this case, upon yet another principle, namely: Taxes for public purposes become increasingly burdensome as they travel further from their source; *i.e.,* their burdensomeness varies with the length of the journey they must make before they find their way back into the hands of the tax-payers, and not—*as we might expect*—with the size of the levy. Let circulation, thus defined, be rapid, let it proceed along well-grooved paths, and the people will always be rich and finances no problem—whether their out-payments are large or small. Let that which the people give up[12] fail to come back to them, however, and the constantly-repeated levies, however small, will bleed them white in no time. A state in which that happens never becomes rich, nor is its people ever other than poverty-stricken.

We may draw from the above the following conclusions: Taxes are burdensome just to the extent that the government is remote from the people. The latter are, therefore, burdened least heavily in a democracy, somewhat more heavily in an aristocracy, and most heavily in a monarchy. Thus monarchy is suited only to states that are wealthy, aristocracy to states of middling wealth and size, and democracy to states that are poor and tiny.

The more one thinks about it, in fact, the greater the contrast one sees, on this point, between free states and monarchical ones. In free states all energies are harnessed to the public welfare; in monarchical states some are devoted to public purposes and others to private purposes, so that the former can be increased only at the expense of the latter. The extreme case here is despotism: instead of governing the people with a view to making them happy, it impoverishes them with a view to governing them.

My point, in this background, is as follows: In each region there are natural forces at work that enable us to say: *here* the impact of climate causes the government to tend toward such and such a form, and calls for inhabitants of such and such type.

Regions in which the land is uncooperative and sterile, so that the product is not worth as much as the labor *expended upon it,* should either be left uncultivated and uninhabited, or peopled exclusively with savages. Regions in which man's labor yields nothing beyond a bare subsistence should be inhabited by barbarian peoples: no type of political organization would be possible in such a place. Regions in which the product exceeds the labor expended by a middling amount are suited to free peoples. Regions in which the soil is productive and fertile, returning a great deal of produce for a small expenditure of labor, demand monarchical government, lest the subjects' surplus go unconsumed due to the absence of princely luxury—the absorption of that surplus by officials being preferable to its dissipation by private individuals. There are, to be sure, exceptions to this rule; but since they bring about, soon or late, revolutions that restore things to their natural order, the exceptions actually confirm the rule.

We must always distinguish between general laws on the one hand and particular conditions capable of modifying their operation on the other. Let the entire south be covered with republics, the entire north with states governed by despots: it would not alter the fact that despotism, things other than climate being equal,[13] is suited to warm countries, barbarism to cold countries, and sound polity to *countries in* the temperate zone. I recognize, moreover, that people can agree about the principle and yet disagree about its application. It might be objected, for instance, that some cold countries are extremely fertile and some southerly countries extremely unproductive. There is, however, no difficulty here, save as we fail, in examining the matter, to take into account all the *relevant* relations. One must, as I have already pointed out, bear in mind such matters as labor expended, the vigor and level of consumption *of the inhabitants,* etc.

Let us assume—for purposes of illustration— two pieces of land of equal size, one yielding five units and the other ten. If the inhabitants of the first consume four units and those of the second nine, the surplus products will be, respectively, a fifth and a tenth *of the total.* The surplus for the first, therefore, is to the surplus for the second as the product of the second is to the product of the first, so that the land producing only five units yields a surplus twice as large as that producing ten.[14]

It is, however, unrealistic to speak of twice as much produce *in a northern country;* indeed I doubt whether anyone would go so far as to put the productivity of the cold countries as high, in general, as that of the warm countries. Let us, however, assume equal productivity—with, if you like, England producing as much as Sicily, Poland as much as Egypt, and, further south, Africa as much as the Indies; and let us ignore everything further north. Just think of the different methods of cultivation the assumed equal product calls for in all these places! In Sicily, the earth has merely to be scratched. In England, what an effort must go into working it! Now: where more hands are needed for a product of given amount, the surplus cannot fail to be smaller.

We must take this into account as well: in warm

countries a given number of men consume much less. The climate being what it is, you have to eat moderately in order to keep well: Europeans die off of dysentery and indigestion when they try to live in it as they do at home. "Compared to the Asiatics," writes Chardin, "we are carnivorous beasts—wolves even. Some people explain the moderation of the Persians on the grounds that their land is not cultivated so intensively as ours. I believe the reverse to be true: the country has a less abundant food supply than ours because its inhabitants require relatively less food. If their frugality were indeed an effect of scarcity, the poor alone would live on short rations; in point of fact —I speak in general terms—everybody does so. The amount people eat would, moreover, vary from province to province, according to differences in fertility; in point of fact the several parts of the kingdom are on equally short rations. The Persians are quite proud of their way of life; in order to see how much better it is than ours, they point out, one has only to look at their complexion. And they really do have a distinctive complexion—even, fine in texture, and scrubbed-looking, whereas their Armenian subjects, who live in the style of the Europeans, have a complexion that is coarse and full of blotches—and, along with it, bodies that are gross and heavy."

People's consumption is smaller in direct proportion to their proximity to the Equator. They eat almost no meat *in the equatorial zone:* their everyday diet is made up of rice, corn, curcur, millet, and squash. In India, *for example,* there are men and women by the million whose daily food-bill is less than a *French* sou. Here in Europe, for that matter, we can observe striking differences in appetite between northern and southern peoples. A Spaniard will keep going for a week on what a German eats for dinner every evening. And it is precisely in those countries whose people are most voracious that luxury expresses itself in articles of consumption: in England it means a table groaning under a burden of meats; in Italy they regale you with sweets and flowers.

Further illustrations of such differences, *caused by the influence of climate,* are provided by luxury in raiment. Clothing is at its best and simplest in regions characterized by sudden and violent changes of season. Elsewhere it is merely a form of ornamentation: the very garments people wear on their backs become a form of luxury, the watchword being splendor rather than serviceability. Go to Naples, and you will see stockingless men promenading along the Pausilippeum—in coats made of cloth-of-gold!

The same considerations apply to buildings. Where there is nothing to fear from exposure to the open air, everything goes into magnificence: in Paris and London the emphasis is on warm, comfortable lodgings; in Madrid you find palatial drawing-rooms—with windows that don't close and bedrooms like rats' nests.

A third difference *between hot and cold countries,* not without influence upon the second *of the two to which I have already directed attention,* is this: The foods consumed in warm countries are not only more substantial but also a great deal more succulent *than those consumed elsewhere.* Why do the Italians eat so many vegetables? Because Italian vegetables are fine vegetables—nourishing and good to the taste. The vegetables they eat in France are raised on a diet of water; they are, therefore, without nutritive value, and people pretty much ignore them at meal-times. But they do not for that reason use up any the less land, or demand any the less hard work on the part of the growers. Similarly, Barbary wheats, in other respects inferior to the French varieties, are known to have a higher flour content—as French wheats are known to have a higher flour content than the varieties grown further north. We may infer from this that as you move north from the Equator toward the Pole you find, in general, wheat of lower and lower flour content. And I ask you: Am I not at an evident disadvantage when, from a product equal to yours, I get a lesser amount of food?

I can add to the foregoing considerations yet another, which both flows from and confirms them: Warm countries are capable of feeding a larger number of inhabitants than cold countries, but actually require a smaller number. This increases the surplus from both sides, and is a constant invitation to despotism for that reason—*and another reason as well*: The larger the area over which a given number of people are spread, the harder they find it to rebel: they cannot assemble on short notice, or secretly either, nor does the government ever have to exert itself much to find out what they are up to, and cut off their communications.

The converse is also true: the smaller the territory on which a large population is concentrated,[15] the less likelihood there is of the government's encroaching upon the sovereign: the people's leaders are no less secure when conferring in their dwellings than the members of the government are in their council; the multitude can assemble in the public squares no less quickly than the troops in their garrisons.

The major advantage of tyrannical government is its capacity to act over great distances. The force exerted by a lever is proportional to its length; that exerted by such a government—thanks to the fulcra it establishes for itself out over the country —is proportional to the distance involved. The force exerted by the people, by contrast, is effective only when it is concentrated: when it fans out over a large territory it is dissipated and spent— like that of gun-powder, which if scattered about on the ground ignites only a grain at a time. Tyrants, in a word, thrive in the most thinly populated countries, just as wild beasts have their way in wildernesses—and wildernesses only. (What I have just said does not contradict my statement—in

Book II, ix—concerning the disadvantages of large states. I was speaking there of the government's power over its own members. I have been speaking here of its power over the subjects. It uses those of its members who are stationed out over the country as fulcra, and thus exerts force upon the people in remote places. It has no such fulcra for exerting force upon those members themselves. Thus in the one case a long lever is a source of weakness, in the other a source of strength.)[16]

CHAPTER IX

Concerning the Criteria of a Good Government

THE QUESTION "What is the best form of government?" is, when asked thus boldly, as unanswerable as it is badly put. Or rather it is a question to which there are as many right answers as there are possible combinations of the absolute and relative situations of peoples.

If one were to ask, instead, "By what criterion can you determine whether a given people is well governed or badly governed?" that would be another matter. For that would be a question of fact, capable of being answered.

It is, to be sure, never answered, the reason being that everyone insists upon answering it in a manner peculiar to himself. The subject exalts law and order, the citizen individual liberty. One man

puts a high value upon security of possessions, another upon security of the person. This one pre-
fers a government that makes the people toe the
line, that one a government that lets them alone.
One man wishes crimes punished, another wishes
them prevented. A would like his country's neighbors to fear it, B would like them not to give it a
second thought; A's neighbor is happy when
money circulates from hand to hand, B's makes a
point of people's having bread.

But even supposing agreement could be reached
on all these points, and others like them, would it
get us any further along toward an answer? No
precise yardstick exists by which moral quantities
can be measured. Even if we were of one mind as
to the criterion, then, there would still remain the
problem of how to apply it.

As for myself, I never cease to be astonished at
people's mistaking so obvious a criterion—or rather
at the bad faith that keeps them from agreeing to
it. What is the end that a body politic serves? The
preservation and prosperity of its members. What
the surest sign that those members are being preserved, that they are prospering? Their numbers
and their rate of reproduction.

We need look no further, then, for the criterion
about which there has been so much controversy.
Other things being equal, that government is
unquestionably best under which the citizens—without recourse being had to extraordinary measures,
to naturalizations, to colonizations—reproduce

themselves and multiply most rapidly. And, *conversely,* that government is worst under which the people decline in numbers, and tend to disappear. Enumerators, the job from this point on is yours: count, measure, and make comparisons.

We should be governed by the selfsame principle in deciding what centuries merit commendation from the standpoint of man's well-being. Take, for instance, the centuries in which literature and the arts have flourished: they have been admired far beyond their deserts—by persons who have failed either to penetrate the hidden meaning of their cultures, or to take into account their sinister after-effects. "It was an element of their slavery, but the ignorant called it civilization." [17] Shall we never learn—with regard to the contemptible motive that guided *certain* authors' pens—what the principles underlying their books have to teach us? No! Say what these authors may, any country—even if its name be on everyone's lips— that is losing population is a country in which things are going far from well. Nor does a hundred thousand pound income for a poet make the century he lives in the best of centuries. We must pay heed not so much to the surface manifestations of good order and the peace of mind of rulers, as to the well-being of nations as wholes— most particularly the states with the largest populations. Although a hail storm may well devastate several cantons, it is unlikely to cause a famine. Although rulers may be frightened out of their

wits by uprisings and civil wars, their subjects'
real misfortunes are unrelated to such events: they,
indeed, may breathe most easily at the very times
when men are vying with one another for the
privilege of tyrannizing over them. The calam-
ities and blessings that are truly such in the eyes
of the subjects are the ones that arise out of their
permanent condition: things go completely to pot
only when the yoke bears down on everything and
everybody, these being the occasions when the
rulers, visiting destruction upon their subjects
when and how they wish, "create solitude and
call it peace." [18] Time was when the kingdom of
France, because of fallings-out among the great,
was in turmoil, and the Coadjutor of Paris attended
Parliament with a dagger in his pocket. That did
not, however, keep the French people from being
happy—and numerous as well—in a comfortable
environment that was both free and decent. [19]
Greece, many centuries earlier, flourished in the
midst of the most savage wars imaginable: blood
ran in torrents—but the country was densely
populated for all that. Our republic, wrote Machiavelli, would seem to have thrived upon the
murders and proscriptions and civil wars amongst
which it lived: the virtue of its citizens, their
mores, their independence, did more to strengthen
it than all those conflicts did to weaken it. A little
excitement gives vigor to men's souls. And it is
freedom, rather than peace, that causes the race
to prosper. [20]

CHAPTER X

Concerning the Corrupt Forms of
        Government, and the Latter's
        Tendency To Degenerate

Just as the private will *of individuals* is always running counter to the general will, so the government is forever exerting itself against the sovereign; and as the government's pressure upon the sovereign increases the constitution deteriorates. There is, moreover, no corporate will of the sovereign to check and balance that of the prince; and, that being the case, the prince inevitably gets the upper hand, sooner or later, over the sovereign, and *thus* breaks the social contract.

There you have the inherent and inescapable vice of bodies politic: from the moment at which they are born it works incessantly to destroy them— much as old age and death accomplish the ultimate destruction of the human body.

A government is corrupted, generally speaking, in one of two ways: either by shrinkage, or by the dissolution of the state *of which it is a part.*

A government shrinks when, in conformity with its natural tendency, it moves from a larger number *of members* to a smaller, *i.e.,* from democracy to aristocracy and from aristocracy to monarchy. A conspicuous example of this process is the gradual formation and development, there among its lagoons, of the republic of Venice.[21] More than twelve hundred years of history, surprising as it may seem, have apparently carried the Venetians no further than the second stage of the process—which began with the Serrar di Consiglio in 1198. The ancient dukes, who are sometimes brought up against them, were demonstrably not—despite the "Squittino della libertà veneta"—in any sense their sovereigns.

Someone is certain to object here that the Roman republic moved in precisely the opposite direction —from monarchy to aristocracy and from aristocracy to democracy. I am far from ready to adopt this view. What Romulus set up to begin with was a mixed form of government, which speedily degenerated into a despotism. The state, for reasons peculiar to itself, perished prematurely—like the not-infrequent spectacle of the newborn babe who dies without having become a man. The republic's real beginnings date back to the time when the Tarquins were expelled. It did not, however, immediately assume a stable form, the reason being that the patriciate had not yet been abolished—which meant that half the job remained to be done. For, that being the case, it remained for the worst of the lawful forms of government, hereditary aristocracy, to fight it out with democracy: the government thus continued to be fluid and indeterminate in form, and, as Machiavelli has shown, did not take final shape until the trib-

unate was established—at which time a real government, and a genuine democracy as well, first came
into being. From then on the people performed
not only the functions of the sovereign, but those
of prince and judge as well; the senate, whose task
it was to moderate the government, or pull it together, was merely a subordinate agency; and,
within Rome's city limits, even the consuls—though
patricians and chief magistrates and, in time of
war, generals with unlimited powers—were merely
popularly-elected presidents. After that turning-
point, in other words, one can see the government—in accordance with its natural bent—moving
sharply in the direction of aristocracy. The patriciate having abolished itself, if I may put it so,
the aristocratic element in the government ceased
to be a class of patricians (as it is in Venice and
Genoa), and became instead a senate, made up of
both patricians and plebeians—or, if you prefer, a
tribunate, once the tribunes had begun to usurp
active power. Facts are not altered by the words we
apply to them, and you have an aristocratic form
of government wherever the people have officials,
whatever the title they bear, do their governing for
them.

The civil wars and the triumvirate were a result
of the corruption of aristocracy. Sulla and Julius
Caesar and Augustus all became real monarchs
de facto, and the state finally dissolved under the
despotism of Tiberius. Thus Roman history rather

confirms than disproves the principle I have put forward.[22]

If the government were to move from a smaller number to a larger we might say that it had "expanded." Any such reverse-order development is, however, out of the question. The fact is that no government ever changes into a new form until —the spring that drives it having run down—it is too weak to retain its old one. Now: If it expanded at such a time it would weaken itself still further. Its strength, that is to say, would be reduced to nothing, and it would be even less able to keep itself alive than it was before. What it must do, then, is wind up and tighten the spring as rapidly as it runs down. If it fails to do this the result will be the downfall of the state, which it is its task to maintain.

Dissolution of the state can come about in either of two ways:

1) The prince may cease to govern the state in accordance with the laws; *i.e.*, it may usurp the power of the sovereign. Where this happens, a transformation of astonishing character comes about, namely, shrinkage not of the government but of the state itself. To put this more precisely: the larger state dissolves, and a new *and smaller* state takes shape within it. This new state, which embraces only the members of the government, stands over against the rest of the people as sheer overlord and tyrant. In a word: the moment the

government has usurped sovereignty, the social contract is broken: the plain citizens—each of whom, rightly, resumes his natural liberty—are thenceforth under no obligation to obey; they are *merely* forced to do so.

2) You get the same result when members of the government arrogate to themselves individually the power they are entitled to exercise collectively but not otherwise. This is by no means a lesser infraction of the laws *than the case just considered;* it produces, as a matter of fact, even more disorder, and results, if I may put it so, in as many governments as you have officials—which means that the state, never one whit less divided than its government, either perishes or changes form.

The general term applied to corruption of the *several forms of* government, where it is the result of dissolution of the state, is anarchy. Taking the forms of government separately, *however, the correct terms are these:* democracy degenerates into ochlocracy, and aristocracy into oligarchy. And if I do not add that monarchy degenerates into tyranny, the reason is that "tyranny" is ambiguous, and calls for a word of explanation.

The term "tyrant," which in common parlance denotes a king who, disregarding both justice and the laws, rests his government upon violence, should be reserved in strict usage for the man who arrogates to himself kingly power to which he is not entitled. That is how the Greeks understood the word, which they therefore applied indiscriminately to princes—good ones and bad ones alike—whose authority was *considered* unlawful. The term "tyrant" is, on this showing, interchangeable with "usurper." "All who hold perpetual power in a state that has known liberty," writes Cornelius Nepos in his "Life of Miltiades," "are deemed and called tyrants" (chapter viii).[23] Aristotle, to be sure, draws a different distinction between the tyrant and the king ("Nicomachean Ethics," Book VIII, chapter x): the tyrant governs in his own interest, the king in the exclusive interest of his subjects. The general run of Greek writers, however, used the word "tyrant" in its other sense (as is especially evident in Xenophon's "Hiero")—besides which it would follow from Aristotle's distinction that the world has yet to see its first king.[24]

In order to use different words for different things, I apply the term "tyrant" to the man who usurps kingly authority, and the term "despot" to the man who usurps sovereignty. The tyrant gets around the laws in order to govern in accordance with the laws; the despot puts himself completely above the laws. While, therefore, a man can be a tyrant and not a despot, the despot is necessarily a tyrant.

CHAPTER XI

Concerning the Death of the Body Politic

SUCH, then, is the natural and inevitable bent of even the best-constituted governments. If Rome and Sparta both perished, what state can hope to last forever?

If what we wish is to create a constitution that will last a long while, then let us dream no dreams of one that will last forever. If we are to avoid failure, we must not attempt the impossible, or flatter ourselves that we can give to a structure built by men a permanence that nothing human ever has.

The body politic is *in two respects* like the body of a man: it begins to die even as it is being born, *i.e.,* it carries within it the seeds of its destruction; and it can have a constitution of greater or lesser robustness, capable of keeping it alive over a longer or shorter period of time. Man's constitution, however, is the product of nature, the state's the product of art—which is to say that man does not have it within his power to lengthen the span of his own life but can, within the limits of the possible, lengthen the span of the state's by giving to it the best constitution it is capable of having. The best constituted state will—*I repeat*—one day perish. But failing some unforeseen accident that wipes it out of existence prematurely, it will perish at a later moment than a state that is less well-constituted.

The prime mover of political society is the authority of the sovereign: The legislative power is the state's heart, the executive power *merely* its brain, which controls the movements of its parts. *Now:* The man whose brain is paralyzed does not necessarily die; neither does the man who becomes an imbecile. But once any creature's heart ceases to function, that creature is dead.

The state draws its energies from the legislative power and not, by any means, from the laws. *We must not be misled here by the apparent status of laws handed down from the past.* Yesterday's law is not binding today at all; what happens is, rather, that the silence of the sovereign is considered as tacit consent. The sovereign is assumed, that is to say, to confirm continuously such laws as it does not use its power to abrogate. *In short:* Unless the sovereign itself revokes its declaration, *people assume that* it still wills what it once declared its will to be.

Why then do people show so much respect for ancient laws? For the very reason I have given: we are obliged to suppose that these laws owe their continuance over so long a time precisely to their excellence, and that the sovereign, if ever it had ceased to deem them salutary, would have revoked them—as it has had countless opportunities to do.[25] That is why the laws of any well-constituted state, instead of growing weaker, acquire new force with each passing day: the aura that always surrounds what is ancient causes them, as time goes by, to be held in ever greater veneration. And the converse is true: where the laws weaken as they grow old, what this proves is that the legislative power is no longer present, and the state has ceased to exist.

CHAPTER XII

How the Sovereign Authority Maintains Itself (a)

THE POWER to legislate is the sole power that vests in the sovereign. The latter acts, therefore, exclusively through laws. And since laws are nothing more nor less than authentic acts of the general will, action by the sovereign is out of the question unless the people is assembled.

"The people assembled!" someone will reply. "What a pipe-dream!" A pipe-dream it is—in our age. But it was no pipe-dream two thousand years ago. *What has happened in the interval?* Has human nature changed?

My answer is two-fold: The frontier that divides the morally possible from the morally impossible is less constricting than we take it to be; and the things that hem the former in are our own weaknesses, our own vices, and our own prejudices.[26] Mean-spirited folk, *for example,* flatly disbelieve in great men, and abject slaves greet the word "liberty" with a derisive smile.

Let us determine what can be done in the light of what has been done. I shall not speak of the republics of ancient Greece. But the Roman republic was, I suggest, a great state, and the town of Rome a big town. Its last census gave it 400,000 arms-bearing citizens. And the last enumeration for the empire as a whole gave it—exclusive of subjects, foreigners, women, children, and slaves —more than four million citizens.

What a task it must have been to convene the vast population of that town and its environs in frequent assemblies! It was a rare week, nevertheless, when the Roman people was not convened— a rare week, indeed, when it was not convened more than once. *Nor is that all:* it exercised, over and above the powers of the sovereign, some of the powers of the government: it handled certain kinds of business. It judged certain types of cases. The Roman in his Forum was consequently an official almost as often as he was a citizen.[27]

Nor were the Romans unique in this respect: If we went back to the beginnings of the several nations, we should find that most governments of ancient times, even governments of monarchical form (e.g., those of the Macedonians and the Franks), had similar councils.

However that may be, the simple fact *of such a council's having functioned at Rome* refutes all possible objections *to my thesis*. We are, I think, on solid ground when we reason from what has been to what is possible.

CHAPTER XIII

How the Sovereign Authority Maintains Itself (b)

THE PEOPLE has assembled on at least one occasion and given its sanction to a body of laws, thus fixing the constitution of the state. It has established a continuing government, or made definitive provision for the election of officials. Its task—*i.e., that of assuring the maintenance of the authority of the sovereign*—is not yet finished: there must be—I say nothing of such special assemblies as unexpected situations may render necessary—fixed periodical assemblies that can in no circumstances be abolished or prorogued. To this end the law must, independently of any formal convocation from outside itself, convene the people in full-fledged assembly on such and such a day.

Apart from these assemblies that are legitimized by the mere fact of being held on a specified date, however, no assembly of the people should be deemed legitimate, nothing done in an assembly regarded as valid, save as it has been convoked by officials authorized to take such a step, and in accordance with prescribed procedures. For the call to assemble must itself emanate from the laws.

As for the question whether the intervals between lawful assemblies should be of greater or lesser length, no precise rules can possibly be laid down about that, the reason being that it depends upon such a variety of considerations. One can only venture the following general proposition: the greater the power entrusted to the government, the more often the sovereign should make itself seen.

That is perhaps well enough, someone will object, for a single town; but what if the state comprises several towns? Is sovereign authority to be divided up among them? Or is that authority to be concentrated in one of their number, and the others subordinated to that one?

My answer is: neither the one nor the other, *for two reasons*. In the first place, the authority of the sovereign is an irreducible whole: to divide it is to destroy it. And in the second place, it is no more legitimate for a town to be subordinated to another town than for a nation to be subordinated to another nation. *Why?* Because the essence of political society lies in the coincidence of obedience and freedom, and because the words "subject" and "sovereign," whose meanings are brought together in the word "citizen," are correlative and inseparable.

My further answer is: the uniting of several towns in a single city is always unhealthy. Let those who attempt it refrain from flattering themselves that they will avoid its inherent disadvantages. And let them, at the same time, never put the blame for the shortcomings of their large states upon a man who would have nothing but small ones.

But how are small states to be made strong enough to defend themselves against large ones? Why, in the same way in which the Greek towns defended themselves, in ancient times, against the Great King. And in the same way in which Holland and Switzerland have lately defended themselves against the House of Austria.

If cutting the state down to reasonable size is out of the question, there remains, in any case, one other possibility, namely: do without a capital altogether, and have the towns take turns at being the seat of government and the place of assembly for the country's states-general.

Distribute your population evenly over your territory. Guarantee the same rights on every square foot of it. Bring abundance and activity to its remotest corners—do these things, and your state will become, as a result, as strong and also as well-governed as it is capable of being. And remember: town walls are invariably built out of the rubble of country homes. I never watch a palace go up in a capital city without witnessing, in my mind's eye, the devastation of an entire countryside.

CHAPTER XIV

How the Sovereign Authority
Maintains Itself (c)

THE INSTANT the people is lawfully assembled as a sovereign body, the government ceases
to have jurisdiction over anything whatever: All
executive power is suspended, so that the person
of the highest official of the land is thereafter no
more sacrosanct or inviolable than that of the
meanest citizen. For the representative, once he
stands in the presence of the represented, represents
no longer.

The disorders that broke out *from time to time*
in the Roman comitia resulted, in the main, from
ignorance or neglect of the above rule: they occurred at moments when the consuls were only
popularly-elected presidents and nothing more, the
tribunes only speakers (in approximately the same
sense in which this term is used in the English
Parliament),[28] and the senate only a cipher. Even
had the rule been applied, however, it would not
always have prevented the consuls and the tribunes
from running afoul of each other, inasmuch as
their functions overlapped.[29]

The prince has always dreaded these moments
when, its authority having lapsed, it defers—or is
supposed to defer—to a flesh-and-blood superior.

Officials in every age have, therefore, thought with horror of the popular assemblies—the very aegis of the body politic—that bring governments to heel. They have, in consequence, begrudged nothing in the way of pains or objections or pretexts or promises that might keep the citizens from holding such assemblies.

When, *therefore,* the citizens have become acquisitive and lax and cowardly, so that they value their comfort more than their freedom, they do not hold out very long against the redoubled efforts the government puts forth *when an assembly is imminent.* This makes for a continuous increase in *the government's* power to resist, and thus explains why the authority of the sovereign finally vanishes, as also why most cities crumble and perish before their time.

Sometimes, however, an intermediate power is introduced between the sovereign and arbitrary government. To this we must now turn our attention.

CHAPTER XV

Concerning Deputies or Representatives

ONCE serving the public thing has ceased to be the citizens' major concern, once they would rather serve it with their pocketbooks than their persons, the state already stands on the threshold of its ruin. Men are needed to march against an enemy? The citizens hire some mercenaries—and keep to their homes. Attendance is required at the council? They name some deputies—and keep to their homes. They end up, partly because of laziness and partly because of money, with soldiers to enslave their fatherland—and representatives to auction it off to the highest bidder.

The things that bring about the substitution of money for personal services are the following: the hurly-burly of commerce and the mechanical arts, the greed for gain, slothfulness, and the lust for commodities. The citizen yields up a part of his gains with a view to increasing those gains when and as he likes.

Give money, and what you will speedily get in return is chains. The word "finance" is slave language; it has no place in the city's lexicon. The citizens of a state that is really free discharge all their obligations to it with their own hands, none of them with gold and silver. The notion of purchasing exemption from those obligations is so far from their minds that they will, *if necessary,* pay for the privilege of discharging them personally. I for one believe—so wide is the chasm between commonly received ideas on this matter and my own—that corvées are more compatible with freedom than taxes.

The better ordered the state, the more do public affairs crowd private ones out of the minds of the citizens, so that the very incidence of private affairs is a great deal smaller. The reason for this is that the part of each individual's happiness that accrues to him from the common store of happiness is proportionally greater, and that the part he must seek through his personal efforts is, accordingly, proportionally smaller. The citizen of the well-governed city goes to council-meetings as fast as his legs will carry him. Under a bad government, *by contrast,* every last citizen begrudges the steps that carry him toward the meeting-place, for the following reasons: *(a)* the business transacted there excites nobody's interest, *(b)* the citizen knows beforehand that the general will is not going to prevail, and, finally *(c)* everyone's time is completely mortgaged to his domestic concerns. Good laws make for better laws, bad laws for worse ones. And you can write any state off as lost as of the moment when some citizen, in speaking of its affairs, asks the question: "What difference does it make to me?"

But for the cooling-off of love of country, the play of private interest, and the vast territorial extension of *modern* states, but for wars of conquest, but for the tendency of governments to degenerate, no one would ever have invented the expedient of *sending* deputies or representatives of the people to the nation's assemblies. In a certain country *I could name,* they have the effrontery to call these deputies—or representatives—of the people the "Third Estate," thus assigning first and second priority to the interests of two classes and third priority to the public interest.

Sovereignty cannot be represented—for the same reason that it cannot be alienated. Its essence is the general will, and for a will to be represented is out of the question: either we are dealing with it, or with something other than it,[30] there is no third possibility. And it follows from this that the people's deputies do not and cannot represent it: they are merely the people's agents, and as such can make no definitive decisions about anything. *In a word:* Any law that the people has not been present to sanction is without effect—is, indeed, not a law at all. *It is this point that they overlook in England.* The English people thinks itself free, but is badly mistaken. It is free only during parliamentary elections: once the members of Parliament have been elected it lapses back into slavery, and becomes as nothing. *Nor is that all:* Loss of freedom, in view of the use it makes of these brief moments, is just what it deserves.

The notion of representatives is of recent origin. We are indebted for it to the iniquitous and absurd system of government that held sway during the age of feudalism—a system under which humankind is degraded and the title "man" held in dishonor. The people had no representatives in the ancient republics—or in the ancient monarchies, for that matter; they did not even have a word for them. The Roman tribunes were regarded with great reverence; let us remember, however, that it never occurred to anyone that they were capable of taking over the functions of the people—and that the tribunes themselves—despite the size of the multitude in whose midst they performed their own functions—never once attempted to pass a plebiscite on their own responsibility. Yet we have only to look at what happened at the time of the Gracchi, when some of the citizens cast their votes from the rooftops, in order to see that that multitude posed vexatious problems.

In a word: Where men value law and freedom to the exclusion of all else, difficulties count for nothing. The wise people of whom we have been speaking kept everything in its proper place: it let its lictors do things that its tribunes would never have dared to do, and had no fear that they would seek to represent it either.

As for the sense in which the tribunes did represent the Roman people on certain occasions, we have, in order to explain it to ourselves, only to think of the way in which the government represents the sovereign. The law being neither more nor less than an expression of the general will, it clearly follows that the people cannot be represented as regards the *exercise of* legislative power. As regards the *exercise of* executive power, on the other hand, this being exclusively a matter of putting force behind the law,[31] it can—and should —be represented.

All this goes to show that one would, upon

making a careful survey, find that there are very few nations with laws. Be that as it may, this much is beyond question: the tribunes, possessing as they did not an iota of executive power, could not represent the Roman people in virtue of the powers attaching to their office, but rather through encroachment—and only through encroachment—upon the powers of the senate.

In the typical Greek republic everything the people had to do it did for itself. It was assembled all the time. It lived in a mild climate, and was not acquisitive. It had slaves to do its chores for it. Freedom was its full-time occupation. How are we, who do not enjoy the same advantages,[32] to keep alive the powers they exercised? *I reply:* Our tougher climates do indeed give us needs in greater number (for the people of a cold country to imitate Oriental luxury and indolence is to will for itself the chains the Orientals wear; it is to accept chains that are even more necessary than those of the Orientals.)[33] During six months out of every year our public squares are unusable. Our flat languages cannot be made intelligible out-of-doors. We value our profits above our freedom. Poverty holds greater terrors for us than slavery.

What then! Can freedom be kept alive only where it is supported by slavery? That may well be the case: The two extremes do *sometimes* overlap. All things that are wholly outside nature have their shortcomings, and civil society more of them than all the rest put together. There are unhappy situations in which some can continue to enjoy freedom only if others forego it—in which the citizen can be completely free only if the slave is deeply enslaved. That is how it was in Sparta. As for the peoples of our own day, what I have to say to them is this: You are indeed not slaveholders, but you are slaves yourselves. You buy with your own freedom the freedom of *those who might have been your* slaves. It is idle for you to boast of the choice you have made, for I see in it more cowardice than humanity.

I do not by any means conclude from all this that having slaves is necessary—or, since I have proved the opposite, that the right of slavery is *ever* a legitimate right. I am merely explaining why modern peoples who regard themselves as free do have representatives, and ancient peoples did not. Be all that as it may, however, the moment a people gives itself representatives it ceases to be free; it ceases, indeed, to exist.

My view, all things considered, is this: only if the city is very small can the sovereign possibly retain, in our day, the powers that belong to it. If the city is very small, however, it will be conquered? Not at all. I shall show later how it is possible to combine the external power of a numerous people with the simple polity and good order of the tiny state. (This is what I had originally intended to do in the later chapters of the present work when, in dealing with foreign

affairs, I came to the problem of confederations—
an entirely new subject, and one whose principles
have yet to be established.)[34]

CHAPTER XVI

The Institution of the Government
Emphatically Not a Contract

ONCE the legislative power has been firmly
established, the next task is to make similar provision for the executive power. This latter power,
operating as it does exclusively through particular
acts, is essentially different from the former, and
therefore calls, in the nature of the case, for
separate handling.

Even if it were possible to lodge the executive
power in the sovereign qua sovereign, doing so
would blur the distinction between law and fact
to such an extent that nobody would be able to
say what was law and what was not—so that the
political society *attempting the experiment,* having
been thus twisted out of its natural pattern, would
speedily fall victim to precisely the kind of violence
it was instituted to prevent.

Under the terms of the social contract all the
citizens are equals. All, therefore, can prescribe
what all are to do, but no one has the power to
require of another any action that he himself does

not perform. The power to require such actions is, however, indispensable to the life and activity of a political society. And it is precisely this power that the sovereign, in instituting the government, conveys to the prince.

Some writers have argued that the act by which the government is established is a contract between the people as one party and the governors it sets over itself as the other. They have argued also that this contract sets up between the two the terms on which the one accepts an obligation to give orders and the other an obligation to obey them. I am sure the reader will agree that this is a strange kind of contract to be entering into. Let us consider, nevertheless, whether this view of the matter can be sustained.

In the first place, it is no more possible for the authority of the sovereign to be limited than for it to be alienated: limit it, and you destroy it. For the sovereign to set a superior over itself, *therefore,* is not only an absurdity but also a contradiction in terms. In obligating itself to obey a master it— *or, to be more precise, each of its members*—recovers its full freedom.

Again: This contract between the people on the one hand and such and such persons on the other would evidently be a particular act. For it to be either a law or an act of sovereignty is, therefore, out of the question. And from this it follows that such a contract would be illegitimate.

Still again: the contracting parties would evidently stand over against one another without any law above them save the law of nature, and *thus* without anything whatever to enforce their reciprocal engagements—which is as different from civil society as anything could be.

The party that has force at his disposal would always decide for himself whether to live up to the terms *of the so-called contract*. We might equally well apply the term "contract," then, to that which happens when one man says to another: "I convey to you all my goods, on condition that you shall give them back to me in any amount that strikes your fancy."

The state has room for one contract and only one, namely, the act of association itself. That contract ipso facto prohibits all further contracts, so that a *further* public contract that would not violate the original one is inconceivable.

CHAPTER XVII

Concerning the Institution of the Government

IN WHAT TERMS, then, must we conceive the act by which the government is instituted?

Let me point out, first of all, that it is a complex act: *i.e.,* it can be broken down into two stages, namely: *(a)* the sanctioning of the *necessary* law, and *(b)* the execution of that law.

The first of these two acts, performed by the sovereign, decrees that there shall be a governing body, as also that it shall be established in this or that form. This act, manifestly, is a law.

The second, performed by the people, names the officials who are to be responsible for the government thus established. Now: the appointment of these officials is a particular act, and therefore is not—*and cannot be*—another law. It is merely a consequence of a law already sanctioned, and, *strangely enough,* is itself essentially governmental.

The point that is difficult to grasp, in this connection, is the following: how it is possible to have a governmental act *performed* before the government has even begun to exist? *In other words:* How is it possible for the people, which *as we know* is now sovereign and now subject, to become, in certain circumstances, the prince, *i.e.,* the magistracy?

Here we run up against another of those astonishing properties of political society that enable it to harmonize within itself processes that seem to be mutually incompatible. It does so, in the present instance, by suddenly translating sovereignty into democracy—with the result that the citizens—made over into magistrates, without however any perceptible change having taken place, in virtue merely of a new relation of all to all—move from general acts to particular ones, and from legislation to execution.

The metamorphosis just described is by no means a speculative subtlety of which there exists no practical example. It takes place every day in the Parliament of England, where the lower chamber transforms itself from time to time into a so-called "committee of the whole house"—so that what was a sovereign court a moment since stands reduced to a mere commission *thereof*. It does this in order to discuss its business in a more satisfactory manner; and it is customary for this commission to report back to itself subsequently qua House of Commons the steps it has just taken qua committee of the whole house, and then proceed to reconsider, under one of its titles, what it has already decided under the other.

The peculiar virtue of a democratic form of government lies in the fact that it can be brought into existence by a simple act of the general will. The *resulting* provisional government subsequently either *(a)* itself remains in possession, which is what it does if a democratic form of government has been provided for, or *(b)* sets up, in the name of the sovereign, whatever form of government has been provided for by law. Nothing has been done that is in any sense irregular; nor is there any other method by which it is possible to establish a government legitimately, *i.e.,* in conformity with the principles set forth above.

CHAPTER XVIII

A Means of Forestalling Usurpations by the Government

THE FOREGOING demonstrations confirm what I have said in chapter xvi above, and justify the following conclusions:

a) the act by which the government is established is a law, and emphatically not a contract;

b) the depositaries of the executive power are the people's agents, and emphatically not its overlords;

c) the people is free to appoint them or remove them as it sees fit;

d) their credentials run in terms of obeying instructions, not making contracts; and

e) when they accept responsibility for the functions imposed upon them by the state, they do no more than discharge a duty they have as citizens; by no stretch of the imagination are they entitled to bargain about terms.

The people, for instance, chooses to establish a government that is hereditary—perhaps a monarchy, which it lodges in a family, perhaps an aristocracy, which it lodges in a class of citizens. It is not, on our showing, binding itself in any way. It is merely giving the government such and such a provisional form, pending the moment at which it may see fit to hand down other instructions.

Changes of the kind contemplated in the preceding sentence are, to be sure, always a risky business, which is to say that we shall be well-advised to leave an established government alone until such time as its continuance is no longer compatible with the public good. This counsel, however, is a purely political rule-of-thumb, and not by any means a principle of right. The state is as little obligated to leave civil authority in the hands of its present rulers as it is to leave military authority in the hands of its present generals.

Let us concede this also: we cannot, when a change of government is in prospect,[35] be too circumspect about procedural formalities. Such formalities make all the difference between seditious tumult and legal propriety—between an outburst on the part of a faction and the recording of its will by a whole people. On this point above all, therefore, we must, when the "odious case" presents itself *(i.e., the case in which a right is claimed whose exercise is dangerous),* permit nothing that strict construction of the law enables us to withhold.

This obligation *on our part* unquestionably confers a considerable advantage on a prince that would retain its powers against popular opposition and yet have nobody able to say that it has usurped them. The prince, that is to say, can easily extend its powers while keeping up the appearance of remaining within them, and can— on the pretext of protecting the public peace— prevent the assemblies whose task it would be to restore good order. By pointing to the silence that it permits nobody to break, and the irregular acts that it has caused to be performed, it can attribute to itself the support of all whose tongues are stilled by fear, and punish all who dare to raise their voices. This is precisely the technique the decemvirs employed when—having been elected in the first instance for one year and then continued in office for a second—they sought to keep the comitia from sitting, and so retain their powers for an indefinite period. All governments everywhere, once state power is in their hands, seize upon this simple means in order to usurp, soon or late, the authority of the sovereign.

The periodic assemblies of which I have spoken above tend to prevent, or at least postpone, the evil here in question. This is especially true if they do not require formal convocation: there is then no way for the prince to prevent them without openly declaring itself an infractor of the laws and an enemy of the state.

The sole function of these assemblies is that of preserving the social contract. They should always be opened by the putting of two questions (there should be a separate vote on each, and in no circumstances whatever should either be omitted):

First: "Does it please the sovereign to retain the present form of government?"

And second: "Does it please the people to leave the administration in the hands of those who are now responsible for it?"

I take for granted here a proposition that I believe to have been demonstrated above, namely this: the state knows no laws that are basic in the sense that they cannot be revoked—not even the social contract. If, then, all the citizens were to assemble and resolve unanimously to break the contract, it would be impossible for anyone to raise questions as to whether it had been broken in a fully lawful manner. Grotius *himself* goes so far as to argue that each individual is free to renounce the state to which he belongs and, providing he leaves the country, repossess both his natural freedom and his property. *(I agree, but would name this further condition:* Provided, naturally, that the individual does not, by leaving the country, side-step his duties, and exempt himself from service to his fatherland just when he is needed; for that would be desertion not withdrawal, thus a punishable crime.)[36] And to maintain that all the citizens together are incapable of doing what each can do separately would be absurd.

BOOK FOUR

CHAPTER I

The General Will Indestructible

A NUMBER of men assembled together have a single will, looking to their common preservation and general well-being, just to the extent that they think of themselves as a single body. The state, where men do so think of themselves, draws its energies from sources that are potent and pure; its principles are clear and unmistakable. It contains no interests that get in one another's way, or conflict. The common good reveals itself plainly so that nobody with a little good sense can possibly fail to see it. *It offers, in a word, maximum guarantees against error on the part of the general will.*

Peace and unity and equality are not friendly to sharp practice in the body politic. Men who are simple and upright are hard to deceive—because of their very simplicity: neither empty promises nor elaborate pretences take them in; they are not clever enough even to be dupes. In the world's happiest nation we can see the peasants gather in little groups under their oak trees to dispatch their affairs of state, and conduct themselves with unfailing wisdom. How then can we help despising

the refinements practiced by all other nations—
which make themselves illustrious and miserable
with so much method and so much secrecy?

A state governed in the manner just described
requires very few laws. When with time new
laws need to be promulgated, the need is apparent
to all: the first man to propose such a law merely
says what each has on the tip of his tongue.[1] It is
merely a question of translating into law what
each has already resolved to do as soon as he has
satisfied himself that others will do as much. There
is, therefore, no need for intrigues—or eloquence
either.

The reason our political theorists go astray is
the following: All the states they see were badly
constituted to begin with, and they are struck by
the fact that no polity of the kind I have described
could possibly be kept going within those states.
They tell over to themselves, with vast amuse-
ment, all the absurdities that a crafty scoundrel or
spell-binder could pass off on the people of Paris
or London. They do not realize that the people of
Berne would have shut Cromwell up in a mad-
house, and that the Genevese would have used a
cat-of-nine-tails on the Duke of Beaufort.

Let us suppose now a state in which the social
bond has begun to wear thin. It has, we assume,
entered upon its decline: particular interests have
begun to make themselves felt in it, and narrower
associations to affect the decisions of the wider
group. The common interest, *in such a state,* is

clouded over, and encounters opposition: votes
cease to be unanimous; the general will is no
longer the will of everybody; there are arguments
and debates; even the wisest counsel becomes a
bone of contention before it prevails.

Let us suppose, finally, a state that is on the
point of disintegrating: all that remains of it is
an empty shadow. The social bond, we assume,
has snapped within every heart, and even the most
unworthy interest now wraps itself insolently in
the sacred mantle of the public good. In such a
state, the general will is silenced: its members
make a secret of the motives that prompt their
actions, and the thoughts they do express are as
little the thoughts of citizens as ever they would
have been had the state not existed; iniquitous
decrees, with some sectional interest as their sole
object, are dishonestly passed off as laws.

Does all this justify the conclusion that the
general will is extinguished, or at least perverted?
No, it remains what it was before: constant, in-
corruptible, pure, although shunted into second
place by other wills, for which it is no longer a
match. The citizen, as he draws a distinction between his private interest and the common interest, recognizes that it is impossible for him to
separate them completely: he simply feels that his
share of the public hurt *he is causing* is negligible
by comparison with the exclusive good that he
proposes to get for himself. Save when this private
good is in question, he not only wills the common

good as his own, but wills it quite as strongly as anyone else. Not even when he sells his vote for money does he drive the general will out of his heart; he merely places himself beyond its reach. His error is that of changing the form of the question put to him, and of offering a reply different in kind from that which is expected; *i.e.,* he uses his vote to say "It is in the interest of such and such a man or such and such a faction that this or that proposal be approved," where what he should say with it is "It is in the interest of the state. . . ." Thus the real purpose of the procedural rules of public assemblies[2] is less that of keeping the general will alive than that of making sure that certain questions shall never fail to be put to it, and that it shall never fail to reply.

I might venture at this point numerous observations on the citizens' rudimentary right to vote on every act of the sovereign. This nothing can take away from them, any more than their right to express opinions, offer proposals, disagree, and discuss—the latter being a right that the government is always at great pains to reserve for its members. This important problem would, however, require a separate book. I cannot possibly squeeze everything I have to say into this one.

CHAPTER II

Concerning the Vote

For a reasonably accurate index both of
the health of a body politic and the present state
of its mores we can, as we have just seen, look to
the manner in which it dispatches public business.
In so far as harmony prevails in its assemblies, *i.e.,*
in so far as the members are able to see eye to
eye,[3] *we know that* the general will is to that extent supreme. If, on the other hand, debates drag
themselves out, if counsels are divided, if voices
are raised, this heralds the ascendancy of private
interests and the decline of the state.[4]

The above is less easy to see where the constitution embraces two or more orders—in Rome,
for instance, where the comitia, even during the
Republic's finest days, were often torn by clashes
between the patricians and the plebeians. This exception to the rule is, however, rather apparent
than real. What you have in such situations, due
to the inherent vice of the body politic, is two
states in one; and if our rule is not applicable to
the two together it is applicable to each of them
separately. Even in the most troubled times, as a
matter of fact, the plebiscites of the people always
went through quietly and by large majorities—

when the senate did not interfere. The people had a single will because the citizens had a single interest.

We also find unanimity where the pendulum is at the other extreme of its arc,[5] *i.e.,* where the citizens have fallen into slavery, and no longer possess either freedom or will: the people, swayed by intimidation and flattery, now acts by acclamation rather than by casting votes; it has ceased to deliberate, and either worships or damns. An instance in point is the shameful manner in which opinions were expressed in the Roman senate in the days of the emperors. This went, on occasion, to ridiculous lengths. One day during the reign of Otho—so Tacitus tells us—the senators were heaping abuse on Vitellius, but took the precaution of making a deafening noise—in order to keep him from finding out, if he ever came to power, what each of them had said.

The foregoing considerations give rise to the principles on which—according as the general will is more or less easy to discover, and the state more or less fallen on evil days—rules should be made concerning the counting of votes and the canvassing of opinions.

There is only one law that, in the very nature of the case, requires unanimous consent, namely, the social compact itself. For the act by which people join together in civil society is, of all acts in the world, the most completely voluntary. Each man having been born free, *i.e.,* his own master, no other man can bind him, on any pretext whatever, without his consent. To maintain that the son of a slave is born a slave is to maintain that he is not born a man.

Let us suppose that, as of the moment when the social compact is made, there are those who oppose it. Their opposition does not invalidate the contract, but merely makes it impossible for them to be included in it; they become, *so to speak,* so many foreigners among the citizens. To reside within the state after its actual establishment, *on the other hand,* is to consent to it;[6] which is to say that all who inhabit the state's territory subject themselves ipso facto to its sovereignty. (This should, in the final analysis, be understood to apply to a state that is free. Where this condition is not fulfilled, a resident may be prevented from leaving, despite a wish to do so, by family *ties,* property, lack of a place of refuge, poverty, or coercion. In that case his mere presence says nothing one way or the other about consent to the contract.)[7]

Apart from the original contract, the voice of the greater number always binds the rest. This is an effect of the contract itself. It nevertheless raises the question, "How is it possible for a man to be free though forced to conform to wishes other than his own?" *In other words:* How is it that the nay-sayers are free, though bound by laws to which they have not consented?

My answer is: the question is wrongly put. The citizen consents to each and every law—including such laws as become law over his opposition, together with the laws that punish him when he dares to violate this law or that one. The constant will of all the members of the state is the general will, to which they owe both their citizenship and their freedom. (Go to Genoa, and you will find the word "Liberty" inscribed over the doors of the prisons and on the irons of the galley-slaves. This is not only a noble use of the device, but a correct one as well: it really is only the evil-doers in each state who keep its citizens from being free. If in any country all the evil-doers had been sent to the galleys, its citizens would enjoy the most perfect freedom.) [8]

When a law is proposed in the assembly of the people, the individual members are not, by any means, asked whether they approve or disapprove of the proposal, but rather this: Does it or does it not conform to the general will, which is their own? This is the question on which the individual expresses his opinion when he votes, and it is from the totalling of *such* votes that a declaration of the general will emerges. If then the view contrary to my own carries the day, that merely proves that I was mistaken, and that what I took to be the general will was not. Had my private opinion prevailed, I should have accomplished a result different from that which I had willed. And if that had happened I should not have been free.

This view of the matter assumes, to be sure, that all the characteristics of the general will continue to be present in the majority. Once they cease to be present, freedom—however the vote may go—is no more.

I have, in the course of showing how private wills are palmed off as general wills in the deliberations of the assembly, given sufficient attention to the steps that can be taken to prevent that abuse, and shall have something further to say about them at a later point. I have directed attention also to the principles on which to fix the fraction of the votes that constitutes a declaration of the general will. A single vote breaks a tie; a single negative vote, and unanimity goes out the window. In between the tie and the unanimous vote, however, there are a number of unequal divisions. And any one of them may, for the sake of the good health and needs of the body politic, be made the required fraction.

Two broad principles can be of use in choosing among these fractions: First, the view that prevails should approach unanimity to just the extent that the decision is weighty or crucial. Second, the required plurality should be reduced to just the extent that the problem in hand requires prompt action. For a decision that must be made without delay, a majority of one should suffice.

The first of these principles is evidently the more suited to legislation, the second to the dispatching of current business. But, however that may be, the two together enable us to arrive at the best fractions to name for declarations *of the general will* by the majority.

CHAPTER III

Concerning Elections

THERE are two ways to go about electing the government and the several officials—this being, as I have pointed out above, a complex act. The first is to cast ballots, the second to cast lots.

Each of these methods has been used in the past by a number of republics. And a highly complicated combination of the two has survived, in the election of the Doge in Venice, into our own day.

"Election by the casting of lots," writes Montesquieu, "is characteristic of democracy." Agreed. But why should this be? "The casting of lots," he continues, "is a method of election that places nobody at a disadvantage: it deprives no citizen of a reasonable hope of serving his country." That gets us nowhere.

Electing officials is a function not of sovereignty but of government; and we have only to keep ourselves reminded of that in order to see why the casting of lots is peculiarly characteristic of democracy, which is better administered in proportion as administrative acts are few.

In a real democracy, public office is not something to be sought after, but rather an onerous burden, which it is unfair to impose upon one individual rather than another. The law alone can impose such a burden—*and even it only* upon an individual selected by lot. All, where this rule is honored, have an equal chance *to escape it;* the choice, *when made,* depends upon no human will; and the law is, in consequence, applied to no particular individual in such fashion as to impair its universality.

In an aristocracy, the government elects the government, keeping itself at full strength by its own actions. The right method for it to use is the casting of votes.

The election of the Venetian Doge does not invalidate the distinction I have just drawn, but rather confirms it. A mixed method of this kind is just the thing for a mixed government—*and I call it that* because it is a mistake to regard the government of Venice as a real aristocracy. There is, to be sure, no participation in the government by the people. The nobility itself, *on the other hand,* is more like a people than a nobility,[9] since there is many a poor Barnabote who has never come within a mile of holding any office, or had anything else to show for his nobility except the empty title of "Excellency" on the one hand, and the right to attend the grand council on the other. The grand council, furthermore, is no smaller than our general council at Geneva; and its illustrious members, in consequence, enjoy no more privileges than our plain citizens. In short—if we put out of mind the extreme disparity in size between the two republics—the Venetian patriciate appears to be the exact counterpart of our middle class,[10] the citizens and people of Venice the counterpart of our natives and inhabitants, and the subjects on the mainland the counterpart of our peasants. On any showing you like except size, therefore, the Venetian government is no more aristocratic than ours. The one difference is that we do not have a ruler who holds office for life, so that we are not under as much pressure as the Venetians to resort to the casting of lots.

In a real democracy—*as contrasted with an aristocracy*—it is election by lot that would be open to little objection. There we should find equality in everything—mores and talents, and principles and fortune as well. The identity of the person elected would, therefore, make little or no difference. As I have already pointed out, however, there has never been any such thing as a real democracy.

When ballot and lot are combined, the former should govern those posts that call for special talents, military offices for example, and the latter those posts, judicial appointments for example, in which the incumbent needs only good sense, justice, and integrity. For in a well-ordered state *at least* these qualities are common to all the citizens.

In a monarchical government both ballot and lot are out of place. Since the monarch is legally the whole government, and the one and only official, the choosing of his lieutenants is his exclusive prerogative. When the Abbé de Saint Pierre proposed that the councils of the king of France be increased in number, and that their members be elected by ballot, he was inadvertently proposing a change in the form of government.

I might go on here to discuss the casting and tabulating of votes in the popular assembly. I suspect, however, that a historical account of Roman procedure in this matter is a better method of driving home the various principles I could establish. It is worth the judicious reader's while to examine, in considerable detail, the way in which public and private affairs were once handled in a council whose members numbered two hundred thousand.

CHAPTER IV

The Roman Comitia

WE HAVE no really reliable documentation concerning Rome's early days. Most of the things people tell about them, indeed, we have good reason to regard as fables. *For example:*

There are writers who say that the name "Rome" is derived from "Romulus." It is in fact Greek, and means force. Numa, also a Greek word, means law. *In a word:* The city's first two kings, when they arrived upon the scene, bore names thus closely related to their subsequent accomplishments. Is this not improbable?[11]

Let me add, as a general proposition, the following: That part of the history of peoples that has most to teach us, *i.e.,* that which tells about their origins, is the part about which we know least. Everyday experience lays bare for us—*to take a single example*—the forces that bring about the passing of empires, *but* no peoples are now a-borning, so that, with respect to the way in which peoples are founded, we have at best only conjectures—*at which, in the case of Rome, we arrive as follows:* From the customs one finds established, we can safely infer that they at least must have had beginnings. In dealing with the traditions that lead back to those beginnings, we can accept as most trustworthy those that are supported by the greatest authorities and underwritten by the most convincing arguments. I have tried to apply these *two* principles in my search for an answer to the question, How did the freest and most powerful people of all time exercise its sovereignty?

The nascent republic of Rome, that is to say the founder's army, was made up of Albans, Sabines, and foreigners. It was divided, hard upon the establishment, into three classes, which for that reason were thenceforth referred to as "tribes." Each of these tribes, in turn, was subdivided into ten "curiae," and each of the curiae into "decuriae" —these being given chieftains called "curiones" and "decuriones."

From each tribe, independently of the subdivisions we have just noticed, they drew a body of one hundred knights, or "equites." These were called "centuriae," and we may assume, since a town has no great need for such subdivisions, that their original purpose was purely military. Even as a small town Rome seems to have had its instinct for greatness, which made it, with an eye to the future, organize itself along lines suited to a world capital.

This original grouping soon posed a problem: Two of the tribes, the Albans (Ramnenses)[12] and the Sabines (Tatienses),[12] neither gained nor lost members. Not so the third (the Luceres),[12] which was the one in which foreigners were enrolled: it grew apace because of the uninterrupted stream of newcomers, and soon left the other two far behind. The scheme Servius hit upon for dealing with this unfortunate development[13] was that of dividing up the population in accordance with a new principle: *i.e.,* he abolished the existing racial division, and replaced it with one based upon sections of the town, each to be the home of one of the tribes; and instead of three tribes he provided four, each of which was to occupy—and bear the name of—one of Rome's hills. In addition to correcting the existing imbalance, therefore, he took precautions against its recurrence; and, to make the new division personal as well as territorial, he forbade migration from one section to another, thus making it difficult for the several races to intermingle.

He also doubled the strength of the three ancient centuries of equites, retaining however the same old names, and created twelve new ones—a simple and sensible device that enabled him, without so much as a murmur out of the people, to emphasize the distinction between it and the knights.

To the four urban tribes we have mentioned, Servius added fifteen other tribes which, because they were made up of people living in the countryside, were described as "rural tribes." Each of these was duly divided into fifteen cantons.

An equal number of rural tribes was added later, so that the Roman people was divided finally into thirty-five tribes. This number remained unchanged down to the last days of the republic.

The distinction drawn between urban and rural tribes produced one result that merits attention—in part because we have no record of anything *else* like it, in part because it made possible the expansion of Rome's empire, and the preservation of its mores as well. The urban tribes might have been expected to arrogate to themselves, before long, both power and prestige, and so quickly crowd the rural tribes into a position of inferiority. But what happened was precisely the opposite.

The early Romans, as everybody knows, had had a marked preference for life in the countryside, having been taught to prefer it by that wise founder who had associated freedom with rural and military activities. This had made the town, so to speak, a place of confinement for the arts and crafts—and for intrigue and wealth and slavery as well. The most illustrious citizens thus lived in the country, and cultivated the land; and the Romans, in consequence, thought of it habitually as the exclusive source of the republic's strength. Everyone, in short, honored the rural way of life because it was that of the most worthy patricians— as everyone preferred the simplicity and hard work of the villagers to the softness and laziness of the urban bourgeoisie. Thus many a man who, had he stayed in town, would have been a miserable proletarian all his life, became, by tilling the soil, a respected citizen. "Our noble ancestors," Varro used to say, "knew what they were doing when they planted their nurseries—the nurseries that were to provide men of strength and courage to defend them in time of war and nourish them in time of peace—in the villages." Pliny, in explaining the honor in which the rural tribes were held, points to their men, and adds that when the Romans wished to degrade a man for being a coward, they transferred him in disgrace to the urban tribes. When Appius Claudius the Sabine arrived in Rome, with the intention of making it his home, he was overwhelmed with honors—and duly inscribed in a rural tribe (it subsequently adopted the name of his family). Newly enfranchised slaves, *as one would expect from all this,* became members of urban tribes, never of rural ones. There is, in the entire history of the republic, not a single instance of a freedman who, having become a citizen, went ahead to become an office-holder.

The principle of all this was a good one. It was, nevertheless, carried at long last to such an extreme that it brought about a change in—or perhaps I should say a corruption of—Rome's political system. *Two things happened: (1)* The censors—after a long period during which they had arrogated to themselves the right to transfer citizens arbitrarily from one tribe to another—adopted the general practice of letting them enroll themselves in whatever tribe they wished. By making this pointless concession they not only deprived the censorship of one of its major sources of strength, but also produced one further result, namely: While the great and the powerful were all getting themselves enrolled in the rural tribes, such freedmen as had been admitted to citizenship cast their lot with the populace, *i.e.,* with the urban tribes. In general, these tribes accordingly ceased to be associated with any particular place or territory, and came, indeed, to be so scrambled together that in the end their members could be identified only on the register. The reference of the word "tribe" thus came to be personal rather than territorial—or, to speak more accurately, it became, to all intents and purposes, fictional. (2) Because the urban tribes lived close by, they in due time often found themselves in control of the comitia, and proceeded *on such occasions* to sell the state to anyone willing to purchase votes from such riffraff.

A word now about the curiae: Rome's founder—as we have seen—created ten of these subdivisions for each tribe. The Roman people as a whole, *i.e.,* the population within the town walls, originally included, therefore, thirty curiae, each of which had its own temples and gods, its own officials and priests, and its own feast-days. The latter were similar in character to the "paganalia" celebrated by the rural tribes at a later period in Roman history, and were called "compitalia."

There being no way to divide thirty curiae equally among his four tribes, Servius chose to leave them alone when he re-grouped the population—thus making them a separate and distinct grouping of the people living within the town, *i.e.,* a grouping entirely unrelated to the tribes. As for the rural tribes and their members, on the other hand, they never had any curiae at all. What with the tribes' transformation into purely civil institutions, and the introduction of a new procedure for raising troops, these units that Romulus had created for military purposes had become superfluous. While, therefore, all the citizens were

enrolled in one or another of the tribes, by no
means all of them were enrolled in a curia.

Servius set up a third classification—entirely unrelated to the two we have already noticed—
which, when judged by its consequences, over-
shadows the other two in importance. He divided
the Roman people into six classes, and defined the
latter in terms of property qualifications rather than
territorial or personal ones—so that the two classes
at one extreme comprised the rich, the two at the
other the poor, and the two in between those of
moderate wealth. These six classes were themselves
divided into 193 smaller groupings called "centuries," so distributed that more than half of them
belonged to a single, *i.e.,* the wealthiest, class, while
one entire class, *i.e.,* the poorest, belonged to a
single one of them. The class with the smallest
number of men thus had the largest number of
centuries, and the class to which more than half
the inhabitants of Rome belonged accounted for
a single century.

Servius, wishing to keep the people from per-
ceiving clearly the consequences of this arrange-
ment, gave it a spurious military twist: In the
first place, he included two centuries of armorers
in the second of the six classes, and two centuries
of fabricators of instruments of war in the fourth.
In the second place, he distinguished, in all the
classse except one, namely the poorest, between the
old and the young, that is, between those legally

exempted from the obligation to bear arms because of advanced years, and those not so exempted—a distinction which, even more than that based on property, made it necessary to take frequent censuses. Lastly, he made the Campus Martius the meeting-place of the assembly, and required attendance—under arms—by everyone of military age.

Servius' reason for not extending his distinction between young and old into the poorest class was as follows: This was the class to which the populace belonged, and the latter were denied the honor of bearing arms for their country. People acquired the right to defend their homes, that is to say, only by possessing homes to defend. Soldiers, in those days, were defenders of liberty. The miserable hirelings who nowadays swell the ranks of royal armies would have been sent packing by any Roman cohort.

Even in this poorest of the six classes, however, one distinction was drawn, namely: between "proletarians" and "capite censi." From among the former, who were small property-owners, the state drew not only some of its citizens, but even, in times of emergency, some of its soldiers. As for those who possessed nothing, *i.e.,* those whom there was no way of counting except to tell them off by the head, it would have none of them. No man before Marius ever stooped so far as to enroll them.

I shall not offer any opinion concerning the merits of this third system of enumeration as such.

I feel safe in asserting, however, that it would have been unworkable but for the simple mores of the early Romans—their disinterestedness, their settled preference for agricultural pursuits, and their contemptuous attitude toward trade and the lust for gain. (Which of the peoples of our day—with their insatiable greed and restlessness of spirit, with their intrigues and their shifts of population, with their wealth always changing hands—could, even for twenty years, operate an institution of the kind without wrecking its political system?) We must also bear carefully in mind, however, the fact that any vicious effects the system might have produced were offset by the mores and censorship together, since both were more firmly established than it— and that the rich man who made an excessive display of his wealth found himself demoted to the poorest class.

Although there were actually six classes, five is the number usually mentioned. We need now look no further for the reason why. The sixth class sent no soldiers into the army, no voters to the Campus Martius; *i.e.,* it had almost no role to play in the republic's affairs, and, *as one would expect,* was almost universally regarded as unimportant. I say to the Campus Martius because that was the meeting-place of the comitia by centuries (Comitia Centuriata). In the other two types of assembly, which were convened either in the Forum, or in some third place, the capite censi had as much influence and authority as the leading citizens.[14]

Such were the several groupings of the Roman people. Let us now turn our attention to the results they produced in the assemblies:

All assemblies convened in accordance with the laws were called "comitia." The usual meeting-place—*as we have just seen*—was either the Forum or the Campus Martius. A given assembly took that one of the three forms—Comitia Curiata *(by curiae)*, Comitia Centuriata *(by centuries)*, or Comitia Tributa *(by tribes)*—that had been specified in the convocation. The Comitia Curiata were the handiwork of Romulus, the Comitia Centuriata that of Servius, and the Comitia Tributa that of the tribunes of the people. Only comitia could sanction a law or elect an official. Every citizen belonged either to a curia or to a century or to a tribe; none, therefore, was deprived of the right to vote. The Roman people was, then, truly the sovereign—not simply in legal theory but in actual practice.

Comitia were legally convened, *i.e.,* their acts had the force of law, only when three conditions were fulfilled: First, the call must have issued from an agency or an official authorized to convoke that type of assembly. Second, the day appointed for it must be one on which the law permitted an assembly. Third, the auguries must be favorable.

As for the first of these rules, the reason for it is self-evident. As for the second, it was strictly procedural in character: it prevented, for example, the holding of an assembly on a day set aside for a feast or market—when rural folk, having come to town to transact business, could ill afford the time for a day in the Forum. As for the third, it enabled the senate to curb the excesses of this proud, spirited people, and place needed restraints upon the zeal of seditious tribunes—who, however, found ways of getting around them.

Decision-making by the comitia was not confined to laws and elections: the Roman people arrogated to itself all the major functions of government. Thus it is not too much to say that the very destiny of Europe was controlled by its assemblies —or that the sheer variety of the business it had to transact was what gave rise to the different forms those assemblies took, according as the decision to be made was of this character or that one.

Passing judgment on these different forms is merely a matter of comparing them with one another. Romulus' intention, in creating the curiae, had been to let the senate curb the people and the people the senate, while he himself kept a whiphand over everybody. He therefore gave the people, by means of this device, all the authority attaching to numbers—as contrasted with that attaching to power and wealth, which he left in the hands of the patricians. In consonance with the spirit of monarchy, however, he gave the edge in this regard to the patricians—the crucial point, in this connection, being the impact of the latter's clients upon voting majorities. The patron-client relationship was a real stroke of genius, by humanitarian and political standards alike; and but for this admirable institution the patriciate, repugnant as it was to the spirit of the republic, could not have survived. The honor of setting such a fine example for the world to follow belongs exclusively to Rome. No abuse ever resulted from it; yet to this day no other people has imitated it.

The curiae continued to function, essentially unchanged, under each of the kings down to the time of Servius (the reign of the second Tarquin being regarded as illegitimate). Thus royal laws were usually referred to as "leges curiatae."

Throughout the republican era the curiae remained confined to the four urban tribes, and continued to draw their entire membership from the populace. For that reason they did not suit the book either of the senate, as spearhead of the patriciate, or of the tribunes—who, though themselves plebeians, spoke for the more prosperous citizens. They fell, therefore, into disrepute, and a day came when the Comitia Curiata's functions were regularly performed—so debased had this assembly become—at meetings of its thirty lictors.

We come now to the Comitia Centuriata, which elected the consuls, the censors, and the other curule officials. What with this grouping's being so heavily weighted in favor of the aristocracy, the difficult thing to understand, at first glance, is why it was not completely dominated by the senate. Of the 193 centuries that made up the six classes into which, *as we have seen,* the Roman people was divided, the wealthiest class accounted for no less than 98; and since the centuries were polled as units, it swung more weight than the other five put together. Thus when its centuries were clearly in agreement they did not even take all the votes —with the result that what this tiny minority had decided was received as the decision of the assembly as a whole.[15] *In a word:* Business was handled in the Comitia Centuriata by counting pieces of money rather than by counting heads.

However, this bias was offset in two ways:

1) As a general rule, the tribunes were members of the wealthiest class; and they—together with the considerable number of plebeians who always belonged to it—provided a counterweight to the patricians' influence.

2) They did not start right out and poll the centuries in their normal order, which would have meant that the first century always voted first. The custom was, rather, to select a century by lot and have it go through the election procedure independently of the others, and then, on another day, to poll the remaining centuries in order of rank. (The century thus selected by lot was called the "praerogativa," *i.e.,* the "prerogative" century, since it was the first to be polled. This is the source of our word "prerogative.")[16] These other centuries voted on the electoral choice of the first, and usually confirmed it. Thus the authority that always attaches to being first was taken away from

rank and, in consonance with democratic principle, assigned to chance.

The practice just described had one further beneficial result: Citizens living in the countryside had an opportunity, in the interval between the two polls, to familiarize themselves with the provisional nominee's record, and thus did not vote in the dark. In the end, however, the practice was abolished, and the two votes were taken on the same day—on the pretext that the elections were consuming too much time.

As for the Comitia Tributa, they were the real assembly of the people. Only the tribunes could convoke them; in them the tribunes were elected, and got their plebiscites approved. Members of the senate did not so much as have a right to be present at their deliberations, so far were they from enjoying a privileged status there—so that they were sometimes obliged to obey laws on which they had not been permitted to vote, and were, in this sense, less free than the meanest citizens. This—the denial of admission to some members—was an injustice, and would have been adequate grounds for invalidating the Comitia Tributa's decrees. It was also entirely without point.[17] The patricians, if they had attended these assemblies—which, as citizens, they had a right to do—would have done so as private individuals and would have had hardly any effect upon the divisions. For votes were counted by the head, the meanest proletarian cutting as wide a swath as a senate prince.

So much for the voting arrangements produced by the several groupings of this great people.

These groupings, in view of what precedes, evidently did not—even abstracting from their results as regards *Roman* hierarchy—by any means come down to pretty much the same thing: each produced results appropriate to the purpose that caused it to be selected *on any particular occasion.*

We may, without entering into too much detail on the issues involved, infer from the above considerations that:

a) The assembly by tribes (Comitia Tributa) was most favorable to popular government, and the assembly by centuries (Comitia Centuriata) most favorable to aristocratic government.

b) The assembly by curiae (Comitia Curiata), in which the Roman populace could swing a majority with its own votes, was favorable to tyranny and mischievous designs. This being the only claim that could be made for it, it came to be held in bad odor—even by the enemies of the regime, who avoided a type of assembly that—*by the mere fact of its having been chosen*—let everybody know what they were up to.

c) The place to look for the full sovereignty of the Roman people was, beyond doubt, the assembly by centuries. Unlike both the assembly by curiae, in which the rural tribes had no voice, and the assembly by tribes, in which the senate and patricians were not heard, it left nobody out.

As for the polling of votes, the early Romans' practice here was, if less simple than that of the Spartans, as simple as their mores in general. All votes were cast viva voce. A recorder wrote them down one at a time. A majority of the votes cast within a tribe, or mutatis mutandis a curia or a century, determined its electoral verdict. And a majority of the votes cast by the tribes (or curiae, or centuries) determined that of the people.

That was well enough as long as decency had the upper hand among the citizens, and the latter were ashamed to be seen casting a vote for an unjust measure or an unworthy candidate. When, however, the people became corrupted, so that votes were being put up for sale, there was nothing for it but to have them cast in secret—thus putting distrust to work as a restraint on the buyers, and making it possible for a man to receive payment for his vote and still not betray the republic.[18]

Cicero, to be sure, deplores the reform I have just mentioned, holding it responsible, in part, for the republic's ruin. I recognize the weight of Cicero's authority on a point of this kind, but cannot go along with him on this one. I should say rather that what sped the Roman state toward its downfall was the failure to carry out enough reforms of this kind. A man who is ailing is not fed the same diet as a healthy man; nor does it make sense to try to govern a corrupt people with laws devised for one that is virtuous. The best evidence we have on this point is the longevity of the republic of Venice, which still exists in recognizable form—for the very reason that its laws were written for wicked men.

As a result of the reform *mentioned above,* each citizen was handed a tablet, by means of which he could vote without anyone's finding out how he was voting. New procedures were laid down—for collecting the tablets, counting the votes, verifying the totals, etc. Nevertheless, the good faith of the officials charged with these functions (the "custodes," "diribitores," and "rogatores suffragorium")[19] was frequently called into question; and while, finally, decrees were promulgated to put a stop to the selling of votes and *other types of* collusion, their very number shows how futile they were.

The Romans were often obliged, in the declining days of the republic, to resort to astonishing expedients by way of making up for the inadequacy of their laws: now an alleged miracle, which turned the trick as far as the masses were concerned but did not take in their governors; now an assembly convoked at short notice, leaving the candidates insufficient time to make deals; now—when it was obvious that the multitude had been won over and was about to do the wrong thing—an entire session devoted to sheer talk. In the end, however, ambition foiled all these expedients.

What is beyond belief is this: despite all the

abuses *noted above,* this numerous people—thanks to the institutions it had inherited from the remote past—went right on electing officials, passing laws, judging lawsuits, and dispatching private and public business. Nor could the senate itself have done these things with greater despatch.

CHAPTER V

Concerning the Tribunate

IF THE CONSTITUENT parts of the state cannot be brought into nice equilibrium, *i.e.,* if the relations between them are constantly being disturbed by forces that it is impossible to snuff out, the remedy is as follows: Set up a special agency, entirely separate from those discussed above, to restore things to their proper position with respect to one another, and to serve as a middle term or connecting link between prince and people, or as a middle term or connecting link between prince and sovereign—or, if necessary, as both at the same time.

This agency—I call it the tribunate—acts as guardian of the laws and of the legislative power. Sometimes—as with the tribunes in Rome—its role is to protect the sovereign against the government, sometimes—as with the Council of Ten in Venice at the present time—to strengthen the hand of the government against the people, and sometimes—as with the ephors at Sparta—to maintain equilibrium on all sides.

The tribunate is not a constituent part of the city at all, and should not possess any legislative or executive power whatever—it is, indeed, the more powerful because it does not. It is precisely because it is itself unable to take any action whatever that it is in a position to prevent any action whatever. It is precisely because it confines itself to the defence of the laws that it is more inviolable, and held in greater reverence, than the prince (who executes the laws) or the sovereign (who legislates them). This is evident from what happened in Rome: the proud patricians, who had nothing but contempt for the people as a whole, had to toe the line in the presence of one of its officials—a commoner, who could claim neither auspices nor jurisdiction.

A tribunate that is wisely-moderated is the firmest support a good constitution can have, while one that has an iota of power in excess of what it should have turns everything upside down. As for its having too little power, that is contrary to its nature: the tribunate, where it counts for anything at all, has the strength it needs as a matter of course.

If the tribunate usurps executive power, of which it is merely the moderator, or if it attempts to hand down laws, of which it is merely the defender, it degenerates into tyranny. The vast power lodged in the ephors did no harm so long as Sparta preserved its mores; once the latter began to decay, however, they decayed the more rapidly because of it. When the said tyrants spilled the blood of Agis, his death was avenged by his successor, so that both their crime and their punishment hastened the downfall of the republic: after Cleomenes, Sparta was as nothing.

Rome moved toward its ruin along the same path: the tribunes usurped excessive power by decree, and that power, in conjunction with laws intended to keep men free, served in the long run to strengthen the hand of the emperors, who destroyed freedom. As for the Council of Ten at Venice, it is now a blood-letting agency, viewed with horror in patrician and popular circles alike, and falls far short of performing its task of nobly defending the laws—so far that it has done nothing since the laws were brought low, except deal blows under the cover of darkness that no one dares take notice of.

The tribunate is like the prince in one respect: it becomes weaker as its membership increases. When the tribunes of the Roman people—of whom there were at first two, then five—sought to double their number, the senate let them go right ahead: it knew it could play them off against one another. And that is just what happened.

Though no government has ever made use of it, the best means of preventing usurpation by this potentially dangerous agency is this: set it up on a non-permanent basis, and specify the intervals during which it is to remain in abeyance. These intervals, which should in no case be so long as to give abuses time to put down roots, could be stipulated by law—in such fashion that it would be easy to cut them short, when necessary, by special grants of authority.

There is, in my opinion, nothing to be said against this device: the constitution, of which the tribunate is not a part, would be none the worse for the latter's eclipse. And it would, in my opinion, accomplish the desired purpose. For the starting-point for a newly-constituted agency is not the power exercised by its predecessor, but that entrusted to it by law.

CHAPTER VI

Dictatorship

IF THE LAWS are inflexible, and consequently unable to adapt themselves to events, then they may prove positively harmful; *indeed* they may, at a critical moment, bring about the downfall of the state. The punctiliousness and leisurely pace characteristic of formal procedures demand an amount of time that circumstances do not always allow. Any number of situations may present themselves that the legislator has failed to anticipate. And to be aware that one cannot foresee everything is to possess a well-nigh indispensable kind of foresight.

In view of the foregoing considerations, no people should seek to stabilize its political institutions so completely as to divest itself of the power to suspend their operation. Even Sparta sometimes put its laws to sleep.

On the other hand, only the gravest dangers can be mentioned in the same breath with that of changing the constitution. The majestic authority of the laws should, therefore, be suspended only when the security of the state is at stake.

In those rare cases in which the above condition is clearly fulfilled, the means by which to provide for public security is a particular enactment that lodges responsibility for it in the hands of the republic's worthiest citizen. This grant of authority may be conferred in either of two ways, depending on the character of the threat:

1) If the danger can be met by greater activity on the part of the government, the latter may be concentrated in the hands of one or two of its members. This does not impair the authority of the laws; it merely changes the way in which they are administered.

2) If the danger is of such character that the apparatus of legality is actually hindering the defense of the laws, one names a supreme commander, who silences the laws and momentarily suspends the authority of the sovereign. In the context of such a danger, there can be no two

opinions as to the content of the general will:
the people's primary concern is, obviously, that the
state shall not perish. Evidently, therefore, the
legislative authority does not cease to exist;[20] it
merely goes into abeyance. The official who silences
it is incapable of making it speak. He dominates
it, but is incapable of speaking for it. He can do
anything except make a law.

An example of the first of these two methods
is the Roman senate charging the consuls, in the
terms of a custom-hallowed formula, to provide
for the safety of the republic. An example of the
second is the naming of a dictator by one of
Rome's two consuls—a practice for which Alba had
created the precedent. The dictator, *be it noted,*
was nominated by night and in secret—on the
theory that to put a man above the laws is a
shameful act.[21]

During the early days of the republic the intervals between dictatorships were brief. The reason
for this was that the state was not yet firmly
enough established to preserve itself through the
sheer strength of its constitution.

The Romans, because of their mores, had at that
time no need for many safeguards that would have
been necessary in any other age. There was no
fear of the dictator's abusing his authority—or of
his attempting to retain that authority when his
term had expired. Such vast powers seem rather—
so eager was each dictator to get rid of them—to
have weighed heavily upon the man in whom they

were lodged. It was as if substituting for the laws was a task painful and dangerous beyond enduring.

My objection to the indiscriminate use of this highest office in the early days runs, as I have already implied, not in terms of the danger of its being abused, but rather in terms of its being cheapened. It could not be lavished upon elections, dedication ceremonies, and other purely formal occasions, without the risk of people's forming the habit—what with the title's being used constantly in connection with insignificant formalities—of thinking it insignificant too. Had that happened, it would have lost some of its power to command respect when it was really needed.

In the republic's declining days the Romans, becoming more circumspect, used the dictatorship with extreme frugality, just as they had formerly used it with extreme prodigality. Anyone with eyes in his head should have been able to see that their anxieties *in connection with it* were ill-founded; that, at this late date, the fact that the capital was weak made it secure vis-à-vis officials at home; that circumstances might exist in which a dictator could defend political freedom and yet not be in a position to aim a blow at it;[22] that, finally, Rome's shackles would be forged in its armies, not in the capital. Marius' feeble resistance to Sulla, and Pompey's to Caesar as well, showed clearly enough what to expect if and when internal authority was pitted against external force.

The Romans' error on this point led them into some enormous blunders—as, for example, their failure to name a dictator on the occasion of the Catalinian conspiracy. The issue at stake, if not purely local, reached no further than an Italian province or two; and this being the case a dictator, with the unlimited authority conferred upon him by the laws, could easily have put the conspirators to rout. Instead the conspiracy was smothered by a combination of happy accidents, which it was unwise to wait for with folded hands.[23]

The senate, choosing not to name a dictator, merely delegated to the consuls such powers as belonged to it. These Cicero exceeded on one point of capital importance—on the grounds that if he was to take effective action he had no other choice. Thus he had no cause for complaint when—having won first-minute approval for his actions, as a result of a wave of *popular* joy—he was called to account for spilling the blood of citizens in contravention of the laws—a charge that could not possibly have been brought against a dictator. The consul's eloquence, to be sure, *finally* swept everything before it; *the fact remains that* this son of Rome loved his country less than personal glory: he *had* sought the safest and most legitimate means of getting for himself whatever the affair had to offer in the way of honors, instead of the safest and most legitimate means of saving the state. He could not have counted on the honors in question, *be it noted,* had he himself proposed the naming of a dictator: he would not have dared to name himself, and could not be certain that his colleague would not name someone else.[24] He was, in short, justly honored as the liberator of Rome— and justly punished as a violator of its laws. His subsequent recall, spectacular *vindication* though it may have been, was, beyond question, *in the nature of* a pardon.

One final point: no matter how this significant grant of power is made, the dictator's term of office must be extremely brief, and incapable of being extended in any circumstances whatever. The crises that cause dictatorships to be established are of such character that the state is either quickly destroyed or quickly saved; and once the emergency is over the dictatorship becomes either tyrannical or useless. In Rome, where appointment was for six months, most dictators resigned before their term had expired; but they might well have been tempted—if they had been appointed for a period longer than that—to make it longer still, as the decemvirs did with their one-year appointments. *In a word:* The dictator had barely time enough to cope with the emergency because of which he had been named, and thus no time at all for dreaming of other projects.

CHAPTER VII

Concerning the Censorship

JUST as the general will expresses itself through the laws, so public opinion expresses itself through the censorship. *To put the same point more precisely:* Public opinion is a particular kind of law, and the censor, as its minister, merely applies it to specific cases—in the same way as the prince *applies the other kinds.* Thus the censorial tribunal, far from being the arbiter of public opinion, is merely its spokesman. Whenever its decisions are at variance with public opinion, they are null and void.

No useful distinction can be drawn between a nation's mores and the objects of its esteem: besides being governed by one and the same principle, they are, any way you look at it, inseparable. *Now:* The last word as to what things a people views with pleasure[25] does not lie with nature but with opinion, so that if you right men's opinions, the purity of their mores will take care of itself. All men, certainly, cherish that which is admirable, or what they judge to be so; where they go astray is precisely in the judging. What we must guide, then, is men's judgment, and—*with men as with nations*—arriving at judgments about conduct is a matter of arriving at judgments about *what to* honor. And in arriving at judgments about what to honor, men take their law from opinion.

A people's opinions take their rise from its constitution. The mores are not, I agree, governed by law. It is, nevertheless, the laws that bring them into existence: when the laws grow weak the mores degenerate. Once that has happened, however, censorial decisions will not accomplish what the force of the laws has failed to accomplish.

It follows from what I have just said that the censorship can be of use when it comes to preserving mores, but not when it comes to restoring them. Your censorship, then, should be established while the laws are vigorous; once they have lost their vigor the situation is hopeless. For when the laws have ceased to have any effect, the time has passed when anything set in motion by them can have any effect either.[26]

The censorship preserves the mores now by keeping men's opinions from being corrupted, now by protecting the purity of opinions by means of wise applications to specific cases, and now—when opinions have not yet crystallized—by actually fixing them: Time was, *for example,* when the practice of having seconds in duels was being carried to ridiculous lengths in the kingdom of France—and it took only the following words in a royal edict to put a stop to it: "As for those who are such cowards as to call upon seconds . . ."; *i.e.,* this judgment, by anticipating that of the public, caused the latter to take shape overnight. But when the attempt was made, also by royal edict though in the teeth of public opinion, to get across the notion that it is an act of cowardice to fight a duel at all, which it certainly is, the public —since it had already made up its mind on the point at issue—was merely amused.

As I have pointed out elsewhere (for the present chapter is merely a brief statement of what I have argued at length in my "Letter to M. d'Alembert"),[27] public opinion does not yield to compulsion. Since it does not, there must not be the slightest hint of compulsion in the tribunal set up to represent it.

We have no contemporary example of this institution; but its skillful employment by the Romans and the Spartans, the latter in particular, deserves all the admiration we can give it:

A man of unsavory character once proposed a wise measure in the Spartan council. The ephors, paying no attention to him, caused the selfsame measure to be proposed by a virtuous citizen. What an honor for the one! What a rebuke for the other! Yet no one had uttered a word of praise or blame to either!

Some drunken revellers from Samos (they were actually from another island, which delicacy forbids me to name in our language)[28] once fouled the ephors' tribunal, and an edict was published on the following day authorizing the Samians to act like boors. No outright penalty could possibly have been so hard to swallow as this withholding of punishment. When Sparta spoke its mind on good and bad conduct, its pronouncements were not subject to appeal anywhere in Greece.[29]

CHAPTER VIII

Concerning Civil Religion

IN THE BEGINNING, men would not hear of such a thing as a king who was not a god, or a government that was not a theocracy. They reasoned *about these matters* after the manner of Caligula. Quite rightly too: only with the deterioration of feelings and ideas over a long period did men become capable of deciding to accept a human being as their ruler, *i.e.,* of persuading themselves that they would not have reason to regret such a decision.

With God stationed at the helm of each political society, there were necessarily as many gods as there were peoples. Two peoples, each regarding the other as different from itself, or even—as was usually the case—as an enemy, could not possibly continue for very long to recognize the same ruler, nor could two armies possibly continue for very long to obey the same commander while locked in battle. In short: polytheism and, by the same token, intolerance—both theological and civil (they come, as I shall show later, to pretty much the same thing)—were the result *not the cause* of the dividing lines between nations.

The Greeks were always rediscovering their gods among barbarian peoples. The fantasy that led them to do this was the product of still another Greek fantasy—according to which the Greeks were the natural rulers of those peoples.

For scholars to be insisting, two thousand years later, upon the identity between the gods of different nations is, in any case, ridiculous. As if Moloch, Saturn, and Chronos, or the Phoenicians' Baal, the Greeks' Zeus, and the Latins' Jupiter, could all conceivably have been one and the same God! As if imaginary beings bearing different names could possibly have something in common!

Suppose someone asked: Why—in view of the fact that each state had its own religion and its own gods—did the pagan world have no religious wars? I should reply as follows: For that very reason. Each state did have its own religion and its own government, and therefore did not distinguish between its gods and its laws. Every war over politics was therefore a war over theology as well, and the bailiwicks of the gods were, if I may put it so, coterminous with nations: the god of a given people had no power over other peoples.

The gods of the pagans were anything but jealous: each contented himself with his slice of empire. No less a person than Moses—not to speak of the Hebrew people itself—gave comfort to this view of the matter when he referred, as he did sometimes, to the "God of Israel."

I do not forget that the Hebrews refused to recognize the gods of the Canaanites. But the Canaanites, a proscribed people, were doomed to be exterminated—besides which the Hebrews were to occupy their territory. When referring to the gods of neighboring peoples whom they were forbidden to attack, the Hebrews used such language as the following: "Wilt thou not possess"—it is Jephthah addressing the Ammonites—"that which Chemos thy god giveth thee to possess? So whomsoever the Lord our God shall drive out from before us, them will we possess" [30]—which, as I see it, clearly concedes to Chamos rights equal to those of the God of Israel. ("Nonne ea quae possidet Chamos, deus tuus, tibi jure debentur?" So the passage runs in the Vulgate. In Father Carrières' *French* translation, what Jephthah asks the Ammonites is whether they "believe themselves" entitled to possess what belongs to Chamos their god. Concerning the force of the Hebrew text I am not competent to speak. I do note, however, that the Vulgate's Jephthah expressly recognizes a right on the part of the God Chamos, while the French translator waters the recognition down with an according-to-you *emphasis* not present in the Latin.) [31]

However that may be, the Jews—first as subjects of the kings of Babylon and then as subjects of the kings of Syria—took it into their heads never to recognize any god but their own. This act of rebellion against the conqueror, for so it was regarded, brought down upon them the persecutions that we read about in their annals; *but* these persecutions are without parallel in all pre-Christian history. Nothing can be more certain than that the Phocian war, despite references to it as a holy war, was not a war over religion. It had for its purpose the punishment of acts of sacrilege, not the subjugation of unbelievers.[32]

Every religion, then, was uniquely associated with the laws of the state in which it was prescribed. Thus the only way to convert a people was by conquering it, and only conquerors could be missionaries. *In other words:* Since the law that governed the vanquished imposed upon them the obligation to change religions, the thing to do— if you wanted to talk to someone about his changing religions—was to start out by conquering him.

This does not mean, *however,* that men *in the pagan world* fought for their gods—far from it. The gods—as in Homer—fought for them, the custom being that each man besought victory from his god, and paid for it with new shrines.

The Romans, before they occupied a town, always called upon its gods to abandon it. They did, to be sure, spare the vexed gods of the Tarentines. But that was because those gods were regarded as subject to those of Rome, *i.e.,* under obligation to do them homage. *In short:* When they permitted the vanquished to retain their gods, it was on the same terms on which they let them retain their laws. Often, *when they did this,* the Romans exacted no tribute except a crown for the Jupiter of the Capitol.

Rome's religion and Rome's gods accordingly spread along with its empire. The Romans, meantime, frequently adopted the gods of vanquished peoples—admitting them, gods and peoples alike, to the freedom of the city. The time thus came when the peoples of their vast empire had acquired, one by one, a vast number of gods and religions, with the result that wherever a man went he encountered pretty much the same ones. That is how paganism finally became, all over the known world, a single, homogeneous religion.

Thus matters stood when Jesus made his appearance, bent on establishing a spiritual kingdom on earth—an enterprise which forced a wedge between the political system and the theological system, and so undermined the unity of the state. Hence the internal divisions that—*as we are about to see*—have never ceased to plague the Christian peoples.

As for the pagans, they simply could not get through their heads this new-fangled idea of a kingdom of the other world. They always regarded the Christians, therefore, as outright revolutionaries, who—behind a hypocritical *mask of* submissiveness—were merely biding the time when they would win independence and power—*i.e.,* cleverly usurp the authority that, so long as they were weak, they pretended to respect. That explains the persecutions.

The suspicions of the pagans were in due time justified by events. The look of things changed: the humble Christians taught their tongues a new language; and the so-called kingdom of the other world stood forth—under a ruler who was not invisible in the least—as the most violent despotism to be found in this one.

Each state, however, continued to have its own prince and its own civil laws. This dual power produced a continuing struggle over jurisdiction, the effect of which was to make a sound constitution impossible in the Christian states. For—because of it—nobody ever quite succeeded in finding out just whom, as between ruler and priest, he was obliged to obey.

Several peoples—including some right here in Europe, or nearby—tried to preserve or restore the old dispensation—but to no avail. The mind of Christianity swept everything before it. Holy religion, *that is to say,* either retained continuously or succeeded in recovering its independence vis-à-vis the sovereign and its autonomy vis-à-vis the body of the state. *For example:* Mahomet, who knew what he was about, tied his political system tightly together. So long as his type of government was maintained, therefore, the Arabs had, *even* under his successors the caliphs, a system that was a single whole, which is to say a good one. In due time, however—having become prosperous, enlightened, well-mannered, soft, and slovenly—they were conquered by some barbarians, whereupon the separation between the two powers commenced to reappear. It obtains, though in a less obvious form than among the Christians, among the Mohammedans today. If the sect of Ali is the conspicuous example, there are other states, Persia for instance, in which the two powers are becoming more and more distinct as time passes.

As for what happened closer home:[33] The kings of England set themselves up as "heads" of the church; so also did the czars. But they did not, by virtue of holding that title, become the church's rulers. What they did become was its ministers—empowered, as they discovered, not so much to make changes in the church as to keep them from being made; *i.e.,* their role in the church is that of prince not law-giver. Wherever the clergy exists as an organized body, it is both magistrate and legislator within its own sphere. In both England and Russia, then, as everywhere else, there are today the two powers, and two sovereigns. (N.B. What makes the clergy a body, *in the sense I have in mind,* is not formal assemblies like those in France, but rather the communion among churches. Communication and excommunication—these are the clergy's social compact. Because of it, the clergy will always have the whiphand over peoples and kings alike. Communicant priests—though they come from different ends of the earth—are fellow-citizens. This is political innovation on the highest level of excellence. There was nothing comparable among the priests of the pagan world, which is why they never became an organized body.) [34]

Only one Christian writer, the philosopher Hobbes, has clearly perceived both the disease and the remedy. He alone has dared to propose that the eagle's two heads be reunited, *i.e.,* that everything *else* be subordinated to political unity—in the absence of which there will never be a well-constituted state or government. He should have seen, however, that Christianity, given its domineering cast of mind, could not keep house with the system he advocated, and that the interest of the priest would in the long run prevail over the interest of the state. What gives Hobbes' political theory its bad reputation is not so much that in it which is shocking and false as that in it which is just and true. (See, inter alia, Grotius' letter to his brother on April 11, 1643, and note those emphases in the "De Cive" of which that learned man approves, and those to which he takes exception. Grotius, to be sure, is so generous that he seems to overlook the good in Hobbes in favor of the bad. But not everyone is this indulgent.) [35]

Anyone who surveyed the facts of history from the above point of view would, in my opinion, find it easy to refute the mutually contradictory theories of Bayle and Warburton. The first holds that no religion is of any use to the body politic. The second insists that that is untrue, and that the Christian religion *in particular* is the firmest support a body politic can have. Our historian could prove to Bayle that no state was ever founded without a religion to serve as its base, and to Warburton that Christian teaching ultimately does more to undermine than to promote the good health of the state. In order to be quite clear about this, I have only to bring into a little sharper focus, as relevant to the topic I have in hand, certain all-too-vague ideas *of mine* about religion.

Just as society is either general or particular, religion, regarded in terms of its relation to society, always belongs to one or the other of two types: the religion of man and the religion of the citizen.

The religion of man has no temples, no shrines, and no rites. It has to do with the purely inward worship of Almighty God and the eternal obligations of morality, and nothing more; it is the pure, simple religion of the Gospels, the true theism; we might call it natural divine law.

The religion of the citizen, on the other hand, is established within a single country, and gives the latter gods and tutelary patrons of its very own. It has its dogmas, its rites, its outward forms of worship prescribed by law: it regards as infidel and foreign and barbaric whatever lies outside the single nation in which it is established; the rights it confers and the duties it imposes reach no further than *the shadows of* its altars. The religions of the earliest peoples were all of this second type, which we might call civil, or positive, divine law.

There is a third type of religion which, by com-

parison with the other two, is an odd affair. It
gives men two sets of institutions, two rulers, and
two fatherlands, with the result that it imposes con-
flicting duties upon them, and drives a wedge between citizenship and piety. We might call this
religion—of which the religion of the Lamas, that
of the Japanese, and Roman Christianity are all
examples—the religion of the priest. There is no
word to describe the mixed and anti-social law that
results from it.

Each of these three kinds of religion, when considered in terms of its effect upon political society,
has its drawbacks:

As for the third, it is so obviously baneful that it
would be a waste of time if I tarried to offer proofs.
Anything that impairs social unity is, *from the point
of view that we have just adopted,* unwholesome.
So also is any institution that sets man at odds with
himself.

As for the second, it is wholesome to this extent:
it draws no distinction between divine worship
and love of the laws; it makes the fatherland the
object of the citizens' adoration, and so teaches
them that service to the state and service to the
state's tutelary deity are one and the same thing.
It eventuates in a kind of theocracy,[36] in which
a man is forbidden to recognize any pontiff save
the prince, or any priests save the magistrates—so
that the man who dies for his country dies the
death of the martyr, the man who violates the laws
is an impious man, and the guilty man who is

publicly disgraced is ipso facto offered up to the anger of the gods: sacer estod.

This second type of religion is noxious, however, in that it is based upon error and upon falsehood. It therefore misleads the citizens, making them credulous and superstitious, and drowns true worship of the Divinity in empty ceremony. It is also bad in that it becomes exclusive and tyrannical, and thus causes a people to become bloodthirsty and intolerant—until finally it breathes only murder and massacre, and deems the slaughter of those who deny its gods a holy act. This makes all other peoples its natural enemies, and greatly prejudices its own security.

We come, finally, to the religion of man, or Christianity. I refer not to Christianity as we know it, but to the Christianity of the Gospels, which is by no means the same thing. It is the religion of the sacred, the sublime and the true: in professing it men—as children of one and the same God—all recognize one another as brothers, and affirm that the society that binds them together is not dissolved even in death.

This religion does not, however, have any assignable point of contact with political society.[37] It does not, therefore, make any contribution whatever to the vigor of the laws: it leaves them, rather, with just that amount of vigor that they can spin out of themselves—with the result that [38] a major bond that particular society can furnish *the state* is not brought into play. Worse still: besides fail-

ing to tie the citizens' hearts to the state, it actually
cuts them off from it—as from all the things of
this world. I know of nothing more at variance
with the spirit of society.

We sometimes hear that a nation of true Christians would be the most perfect society imaginable.
There is, as I see it, only one thing wrong with
this conjecture, to wit: a nation of true Christians
would long since have ceased to be a society made
up of men. I am, indeed, prepared to go still
further and say that this dream-society would not,
for all its perfection, be the most powerful of
societies, or the most lasting either. A perfect
society would be ipso facto a society lacking unity,
a society, *that is to say,* whose fatal defect would
lie in its very perfection.

Let us visualize such a society: Everybody would
do his duty. The subjects would obey the laws.
The rulers would rule justly and with moderation. The officials would be men of integrity,
whom nothing could corrupt. The soldiers would
snap their fingers at death. There would be no
manifestations of vanity, or of luxury either. Excellent, so far. But let us look a little further:

Christianity is a religion of the spirit through and
through; it is concerned with things laid up in
heaven, to the exclusion of all else. The Christian's
fatherland, *for that reason,* is not of this world.
He does his duty, certainly; but he does it without caring whether his efforts meet with success
or with failure. So long as his own conscience is

clear, it is all one to him whether things go well here below or go badly. Let the state flourish—and, so anxious is he lest he take pride in his country's glory, that he hardly dares to share in the general contentment. Let the state perish, and he blesses the hand of God that lies heavy upon his people.

Again: Our dream-society could have a peaceful and harmonious existence only if the citizens were, without single exception, equally good Christians. Let the day come when, to its misfortune, a single man of ambition, a single hypocrite, a single Catiline or Cromwell appears upon the scene—does anyone doubt that he will twist his pious compatriots around his finger? Christian charity does not lightly permit a man to think ill of his neighbor, so that once our Catiline has hit upon some crafty way of putting upon those compatriots, and has got this or that crumb of public authority into his hands—behold a man clothed with dignity! It is God's will that he be treated with deference, so that before long—behold a *man clothed with* power. It is also God's will that he be obeyed. He abuses his power? He is the rod with which God punishes his children—*besides which* we must think twice before overthrowing a usurper. That would mean disturbing the people's peace, using violence, spilling blood, all of which is difficult to reconcile with Christian meekness. After all, what does it matter, in this vale of tears, whether you are your own man or somebody else's? What matters is to get to heaven. And resignation improves one's chances of getting there.

Still again: Our perfect society finds itself at war with an external enemy? The citizens march willingly into battle. The thought of taking to their heels does not cross their minds. They do their duty. But they do it without the lust for victory: they know how to die, but they do not know how to win. Perhaps they will achieve the victory, perhaps they will go down to defeat—does it really matter which? Does Providence not know better than they what is good for them? Imagine them face to face with a proud and vigorous and lusty foe—how he would turn this stoical attitude to his advantage! Set them over against a stout-hearted enemy *from the past,* consumed by a burning love for glory and for fatherland. Pit your Christian republic against Sparta or Rome! Either your pious Christians will be beaten back, routed, annihilated, before they know what has happened to them— or, if their skins are saved, it will be thanks entirely to the contempt they will have inspired in their foe. The oath that Fabius' soldiers swore—a noble one, to my way of thinking—was not an oath to win or die, but an oath to come home victorious—which is what they did. Christians would never have sworn such an oath. They would have thought of it as tempting God.

But I have fallen into error in speaking of a "Christian" republic. These two words are mutually exclusive. Christianity preaches only servitude and dependence; its spirit is too great an invitation to tyranny for the latter ever to fail to take advantage of it. Your true Christians are born slaves.[39] They know this themselves, but—this brief life being of so little moment in their eyes—give it hardly a second thought.

But, we are told, Christians make fine troops. This I deny—indeed I know of no Christian troops, and would like to be shown some examples. The Crusades? I do not dispute the Crusaders' bravery for a moment; but let me point out that, far from being Christians, they were priest's soldiers—citizens of the Church, fighting for the Church's spiritual homeland, which it had somehow transformed into a temporal one. That, correctly understood, smacks of paganism: The Gospels preach no national religion, so that a religious war waged by *true* Christians[40] is unthinkable.

The Christian soldiers fought bravely under the pagan emperors? So all Christian writers assure us, and I take their word for it. But they were competing for honors with the pagan troops—and once the emperors themselves had become Christians the competition ceased. Once the cross had put the eagle to flight, *that is to say,* Roman valor became a thing of the past.

So much for political considerations. Let us now turn our attention once again to the problem of right, with a view to clarifying the principles governing the crucial matter we have in hand.

The power that the sovereign exercises over the subjects in virtue of the social compact certainly does not—as I have put it above—extend beyond *what* the public interest *requires*. And it follows from this, inter alia, that the sovereign is entitled to call the citizens to account for their opinions only to the extent that the latter are of importance to the community.[41] ("Each individual in a republic," writes the Marquis d'Argenson, "is completely free with respect to that which does not injure others." There is the borderline, which never moves; nor could anyone possibly put it more precisely. I have been unable to deny myself the pleasure of occasionally citing this manuscript, despite the fact that it is unknown to the public, because I can, in doing so, pay tribute to the memory of an illustrious and worthy man. His heart, even after he became minister, remained that of a true citizen, as his ideas concerning the government of his country continued to be upright and sound.)[42]

Thus much, however, is of importance to the *community, and thus to the* state: each citizen must have a religion requiring him to cherish his duties. The dogmas of that religion, admittedly, are a concern of the state, as also of its *other* members, only in so far as they relate either to morality or to the duties the faithful are enjoined to discharge toward others. Outside these areas, *that is to say,* each citizen can hold any opinions he pleases, without the sovereign's being entitled to take cognizance of them. The competence of the sovereign does not, in short, extend into the world beyond. Let the citizens, then, be good citizens in this life, and their fate in the life to come—be that fate what it may—is no affair of the sovereign's.

It follows from the above, *however,* that the sovereign is entitled to fix the tenets of a purely civil *creed, or* profession of faith. These would not be, strictly speaking, dogmas of a religious character, but rather sentiments *deemed indispensable* for participation in society[43]—*i.e.,* sentiments without which no man can be either a good citizen or a loyal subject. (Cato and Cicero, when refuting Caesar's plea for Catiline, in the course of which he had attempted to demonstrate the dogma of the mortality of the soul, did not pause to philosophize. They merely proved that Caesar's utterance was that of a bad citizen, *i.e.,* that he was advancing a doctrine pernicious to the state. It was that issue, not the theological one, that the senate had to decide.)[44]

The sovereign can oblige no one to believe these tenets. But it can banish from the state anyone who does not believe them—on a charge not of impiety but of unsociability, *i.e.,* on the grounds that he is incapable of sincerely loving the laws and justice, or of sacrificing his life to duty in time of need.

As for that man who, having committed himself publicly to the *state's* articles of faith, acts on any occasion as if he does not believe them, let his punishment be death. He has committed the

greatest of all crimes: he has lied in the presence
of the laws.

The dogmas of the civil religion should be
simple, few in number, precisely formulated, without interpretation or commentary. The existence of
God—powerful, rational, beneficent, prescient, and
bountiful; the life to come; the blessedness of the
just; the punishment of the wicked; the sanctity of
the social contract and the laws—these are the
positive dogmas. As for negative dogmas, I recognize only one, *concerning* intolerance. For intolerance is characteristic of the religions we have
excluded.

Those who distinguish between civil intolerance
and theological intolerance are, to my way of thinking, mistaken: wherever you find either of the
two you find the other also. One cannot live in
peace with people one regards as damned. To love
them would be to despise God, who has decreed
their punishment: one must bring them back into
the fold, or else make them suffer. Wherever theological intolerance is countenanced, therefore, it
invariably affects civil affairs, and once that happens the sovereign ceases to be sovereign even over
temporal matters. From then on the priests are
the real rulers, and kings merely their agents.
(Marriage, for instance, is a civil contract, with
civil effects essential to a society's survival. Now:
let us assume a situation in which the clergy has
arrogated to itself exclusive power to approve such

a contract—this being a power that the clergy of any intolerant religion must, as a matter of course, get into its hands. Is it not clear that the clergy, in winning this power for the church, will have reduced that of the prince to naught? Is it not clear also that the prince will in future have just as many subjects as it suits the clergy's book to make available? Once the clergy has the last word about marrying people or not marrying them—according to whether they profess or do not profess such and such a doctrine, or accept or reject such and such a formula, or are more devout or less devout—*its future course is mapped out for it:* evidently it has only to conduct itself prudently and stand its ground firmly, in order to get its way with, *e.g.,* inheritances and public employments, *thus* with the citizens, and *thus, finally,* with the state itself, which cannot possibly survive with a population made up entirely of bastards. But, someone will object, there will be appeals on grounds of abuse, postponements, decrees, recoveries of temporal power *by those entitled to exercise it.* How inconvenient! The clergy, however poor its store of good sense if not of courage, will keep hands off and go the tenor of its way: it will calmly let the appeals and delays and decisions and recoveries of temporal power go on and on—and when all is done it will still be in control. Surrendering the part is, I suggest, never any great sacrifice when one is sure of getting the whole into one's hands.)[45]

In our day there is—and can be—no such thing

as an exclusive national religion. We should, therefore, tolerate all religions that are themselves tol-
erant of other religions—in so far as their dogmas
contain nothing at variance with the obligations
of the citizen. I make an exception of those cases
in which the state is the church and the prince the
pontiff. In all other cases, however, the man who
makes bold to say "Outside the Church there is no
salvation" should be driven from the state. That
is wholesome doctrine only where government is
theocratic; elsewhere it is pernicious. The grounds
on which Henry IV is said to have embraced the
religion of Rome should induce any decent man—
above all any prince capable of reasoned thought
—to turn his back on it.

CHAPTER IX

Conclusion

HAVING laid down the true principles of
political right, and tried my hand at providing a
lawful basis for the state,[46] I might have gone ahead
to make the latter strong as regards its external
relations. This term would cover international law,
commerce, the right of war and conquest, public
law, leagues, negotiations, treaties, etc. But that
adds up to a new project altogether, too big for
my myopic eyes—which I should always have kept
fixed on things closer by.

NOTES

NOTES

BOOK ONE

1. More literally: so that justice and utility will not find themselves separated at all.
2. Literally: and.
3. Literally: and once he is of the age of reason, he being the sole judge of the means appropriate to his self-preservation, he becomes thereby his own master.
4. This paragraph is a footnote in original.
5. Footnote in original.
6. Literally: was . . . had.
7. Literally: force is a power, etc.
8. Literally: and what morality can derive from its effects, etc.
9. Literally: such a gift would be contrary to, etc.
10. A literal translation would read: Fights between individuals are acts that do not constitute a state.
11. The lines in parentheses are a footnote in the original.
12. Literally: presupposes no treaty of peace between them.
13. Literally: there always will be, etc.
14. Literally: is.
15. Literally: this difficulty, brought back to my subject, can be stated in the following terms, etc.
16. Literally: by all the other persons uniting.
17. The lines in parentheses are a footnote in the original.

18. Literally: finds himself obligated under a dual relation.
19. Literally: a public deliberation.
20. Literally: violated . . . would annihilate. . . .
21. Literally: without its members' resenting it.
22. Literally: the sovereign, merely by being, is always what it should be. An alternative reading: the sovereign, merely by being what it is, is always what it ought to be.
23. Literally: there would be nothing, despite etc., . . . to answer to it for their commitments.
24. Literally: his absolute and naturally independent existence.
25. Literally: when.
26. Literally: since.
27. Literally: those ceremonies were heaped on top of one another rather pointlessly.
28. Literally: to maintain the poor man in his misery and the rich man in his possession.
29. The lines in parentheses are a footnote in the original.

BOOK TWO

1. Literally: toward preferences.
2. Literally: always.
3. The lines in parentheses are a footnote in the original.
4. More literally: "There is often a great deal of difference between the will of everybody and the general will; the latter looks exclusively to the common interest, the former looks to private interest, and is merely a sum of particular wills."

5. The lines in parentheses are a footnote in the original.

6. The lines in parentheses are a footnote in the original, depending from the first sentence of the paragraph.

7. The lines in parentheses are a footnote in the original, depending from the word sovereign.

8. More literally: changes in nature.

9. More literally: in this institution.

10. More literally: any particular affair.

11. More literally: the competence of the sovereign's power.

12. More literally: Their very lives that they have pledged to the state are protected by it at every moment, etc.

13. Literally: the thing that is conformable to order, etc.

14. The lines in parentheses are a footnote in the original.

15. The lines in parentheses are a footnote in the original.

16. The lines in parentheses are a footnote in the original.

17. The lines in parentheses are a footnote in the original.

18. More literally: both announce even today the great men who drafted them.

19. Literally: touch its diseases in order to destroy them.

20. More literally: a weight gets heavier at the end of a longer lever.

21. Literally: the general authority.

22. Literally: in either of two ways.

23. Literally: to give the state its true area.
24. Literally: is found in that relation.
25. Literally: for the supplement.
26. Literally: so as, favored by public fright, to get approval for destructive laws, etc.
27. Literally: the genuine yoke of the laws.
28. The entire paragraph is a footnote in the original, depending from the words "one which other peoples can get along without."
29. Literally: All these conditions are, to be sure, brought together with difficulty.
30. Literally: that power shall be short of all violence.
31. This and the preceding two sentences are a footnote in the original.
32. Literally: must be modified in each country in terms of the relationships, etc.
33. The lines in parentheses are a footnote in the original.
34. More literally: this relation is composed of that between intermediate terms.
35. Literally: excessively dependent vis-à-vis the city.

BOOK THREE

1. Footnote in original.
2. Literally: and the government.
3. A literal translation would read: We can now say as much . . .
4. The words "Paladin of Posnonia, father of the King of Poland, Duke of Lorraine," are a footnote in the original.
5. In Latin in original.

6. The words between dashes are a footnote in the original.

7. The lines in parentheses are a footnote in the original.

8. The entire paragraph is a footnote in the original.

9. In Latin in original.

10. Footnote in original.

11. The citation is a footnote in the original.

12. Let the little the people gives up, etc.

13. Literally: as far as the effect of climate is concerned.

14. More literally: the relation between the surpluses is the inverse of the relation between the products.

15. More literally: . . . the more a numerous people is concentrated . . .

16. The lines in parentheses are a footnote in the original.

17. In Latin in original.

18. In Latin in original.

19. More literally: from living happy and numerous, etc.

20. The entire paragraph is a footnote in the original.

21. This sentence, the remainder of the paragraph, and the ensuing two paragraphs are a single footnote in the original.

22. The footnote ends here.

23. In Latin in original.

24. Footnote—beginning with the quotation from Miltiades—in the original.

25. More literally: The sovereign would have revoked them a thousand times had it not constantly deemed them salutary . . .

26. Literally: The bounds of the possible in things

moral are less narrow than we think. It is our weaknesses, our vices, our prejudices, that restrict them.

27. Literally: That entire people was in the Forum as often in its capacity as official as in its capacity as citizen.

28. The words in parentheses are a footnote in the original.

29. This sentence is a footnote in the original.

30. Literally: it is either the same, or other.

31. Literally: this being neither more nor less than force applied to the law, etc.

32. Literally: who no longer enjoy such advantages. . . .

33. Footnote in original.

34. Footnote in original.

35. Literally: in such a case.

36. Footnote in the original.

BOOK FOUR

1. Literally: what each has already felt.

2. More literally: The law of public order in assemblies, etc.

3. Literally: to the extent that the points of view approach unanimity.

4. Literally: Long debates, dissensions, tumult—these announce, etc.

5. Literally: Unanimity recurs at the other extreme of the circle.

6. Literally: after the actual establishment of the state, consent is in residence.

7. The lines in parentheses are a footnote in the original.

8. The lines in parentheses are a footnote in the original.

9. Literally: The nobility there is itself people.

10. Literally: our middle class is the exact counterpart of, etc.

11. This and the preceding four sentences are a footnote in the original.

12. Footnote in original.

13. Literally: abuse.

14. This and the preceding sentence are a footnote in the original, depending from the words "Campus Martius."

15. Literally: was received as a decision of a multitude.

16. The lines in parentheses are a footnote in the original.

17. Literally: This injustice was quite pointless, and itself sufficed to invalidate the decrees of this assembly which denied admission to some of its members.

18. Literally: Making it possible for scoundrels not to be traitors.

19. Footnote in original.

20. Literally: the suspension of the legislative authority does not, therefore, abolish it at all, etc.

21. This sentence is a footnote in the original, depending from the word "dictator."

22. Literally: that a dictator could, in certain circumstances, defend public liberty without ever being able to strike a blow at it, etc.

23. Literally: happy accidents, that human prudence should never have been counting on.
24. This sentence is a footnote in the original.
25. Literally: as to its pleasures.
26. Literally: the time has passed when anything legitimate can have, etc.
27. Footnote in original.
28. Footnote in original.
29. The sentence is in the present tense in the original.
30. The passage is taken from the King James version of the Bible.
31. The lines in parentheses are a footnote in the original.
32. This and the preceding sentence are a footnote in the original.
33. Literally: as for what happened among us, etc.
34. The lines in parentheses are a footnote in the original, depending from the word "prince" in the second from the last sentence of the paragraph.
35. The lines in parentheses are a footnote in the original.
36. Literally: it is a kind of theocracy.
37. Literally: bears no particular relation to political society.
38. Literally: a major bond of particular society is not brought into play.
39. Literally: are made to be slaves, etc.
40. Literally: among Christians.
41. Literally: the subjects are accountable to the sovereign for their opinions only in so far as the latter, etc.
42. The lines in parentheses are a footnote in the

original, depending from the next sentence preceding.

43. Literally: sentiments of sociability.
44. The lines in parentheses are a footnote in the
    original.
45. The lines in parentheses are a footnote in the
    original, depending from the words corresponding
    to "affects civil affairs" in the last sentence but one
    preceding the opening parenthesis.
46. Literally: to rest the state upon its base.

TRANSLATOR'S NOTE

IN TRANSLATING *Du contrat social,* I have kept open before me several of the better-known critical editions (Beauvalon, Halbwachs, Vaughan, and de Jouvenel). Where discrepancies among them were of such character as to affect the translation, I have followed the most recent critical editor, Bertrand de Jouvenel, who has given me invaluable assistance with many a difficult passage.

I have taken a number of liberties, which in the present edition I shall merely record, and not try to defend: (1) I have often followed my own notions, not Rousseau's, as to where to begin and end a paragraph or a sentence. (2) I have incorporated all of Rousseau's footnotes, mostly enclosing them in parentheses, in the body of the text. (3) I have suppressed all of Rousseau's italics, in order to make way for my own. The latter, like those in the King James version of the Bible, indicate to the reader those parts of the translation for which I have no—or no adequate—textual basis. Ignore the italicized words, phrases, sentences, and you have a complete "literal" translation of the *Contract*. Include them as you read, and you have either (a) what the sentences concerned actually communicate to me, or (b) my best guess as to what Rousseau was trying to say, and would have said had he written more carefully. In most cases, it is a matter of (a), not (b); the (b)'s I have tried to restrict to passages that simply cannot be fitted into the argument without putting a word or phrase or sentence into Rousseau's mouth.